GCSE PE

For EDEXCEL

Julie Walmsley

Acknowledgements

The publishers would like to thank the following for permission to reproduce photographs:

Actionplus on pp. 14b, 15b, 17, 35a, 36b, 57, 76a, 76b, 102, 123b, 129c, 129e; Ken Kaminesky/Corbis on p. 73a; Duomo/Corbis on pp. 30b, 113; Michael Keller/Corbis on p. 35b; Consignia on p. 13b; Digital Vision on pp. 15a, 16b, 31b, 62, 63b, 110, 123g, 123h; EMPICS on pp. 9, 14a, 16a, 19b, 19c, 30a, 31a, 34, 39, 42, 44, 50, 51, 56c, 56e, 56f, 60, 63a, 64a, 64b, 66, 68, 72, 73b, 74a, 74b, 74d, 77a, 83, 84a, 87a, 87b, 87c, 88, 95, 108, 109a, 115, 123d, 123f, 129a, 129b, 129d, 136a, 136b, 138a; Laurence Griffiths/Getty Images on p. 70b; Shaun Botterill/Getty Images on p. 70a; Mirrorpix on pp. 23b, 77b; Michael Crabtree/PA Photos on p. 54; PhotoDisc on pp. 6, 7, 8, 15c, 18, 19a, 23a, 36a, 49, 56b, 70c, 70d, 79b, 81, 84c, 123a, 124, 131, 134, 135; Don Gray/Photofusion on p. 11; Gary Roberts/Rex Features on p. 43; Rex Features on pp. 13c, 79a; Andrew Syred/Science Photo Library on p. 99; NIBSC/Science Photo Library on p. 100; Oscar Burriel/Science Photo Library on p. 67; Phil Jude/Science Photo Library on pp. 58, 104.

Cover image: Corbis

United Kingdom: Folens Publishers, Apex Business Centre, Boscombe Road, Dunstable, LU5 4RL.
Email: folens@folens.com

Ireland: Folens Publishers, Greenhills Road, Tallaght, Dublin 24.
Email: info@folens.ie

Poland: JUKA, ul. Renesansowa 38, Warsaw 01-905.

Editor: Melody Ismail

Illustrations by Roger Goode, Colin Brown and Maggie Rammage – Beehive Illustration and Mark Stacey.

Cover design: Duncan McTeer

Index compiled by Indexing Specialists (UK) Ltd

Layout by Hardlines Ltd, Charlbury, Oxford

First published 2003 by Folens Limited.
Reprinted 2003.

British Library Cataloguing in Publication Data. A catalogue record for this publication is available from the British Library.

ISBN 1-84303-239-2

Contents

Introduction   4

Section A: Exercise and Training

A1 Reasons for Taking Part in Activity   6

A2 Health, Fitness, Exercise and Performance   12

A3 Skill-Related Fitness   18

A4 Principles of Training   20

A5 Methods of Training   32

A6 Diet, Health and Hygiene (1)   46

A6 Diet, Health and Hygiene (2)   60

Section B: Safety Aspects and Risk Assessment

B1 Prevention of Injury   68

B2 Sports Injuries   84

Section C: Applied Anatomy and Physiology

C1 The Circulatory System   96

C2 The Respiratory System   104

C3 Bones   112

C4 Joints, Tendons and Ligaments   124

C5 Muscles and Muscle Action   132

Analysis of Performance   140

Glossary   156

Index   162

Introduction

The contents of this book cover the theory content for Edexcel Paper 1 *Factors Affecting Participation and Performance* and *Analysis of Performance* from Paper 2. The course content for Paper 1 is set out in three sections.

Section A – Exercise and Training, provides an understanding of why people take part in physical activity, how health and fitness can be improved by applying training principles and methods and how an individual can adapt their lifestyle to gain maximum fitness.

Section B – Safety Aspects and Risk Assessment in Sport and Physical Activity, concerns sports injuries and how they are caused, prevented and treated. Injuries covered range from minor cuts and bruises to major problems such as fractures, dehydration and resuscitation.

Section C – Applied Anatomy and Physiology, looks at how the bones, joints, muscles, circulatory and respiratory systems interrelate to allow for different types of physical activity.

Knowledge and understanding of the topics covered in this book can be useful in jobs needing a level of physical fitness, like working in the police force or fire service. The elements of first aid that are covered may bring about an interest that could lead to a pursuit of the job or hobby involving first aid. In general, the whole course is useful to those hoping to pursue a career in the sports leisure industry, as a coach or as a participant at any level.

The book layout

The book is set out so that it matches the Edexcel specification. The headings of each of the sections and the order in which topics are covered relate directly to the specification. This means that if you carefully work your way through this book you will cover everything that the exam board requires of you. To help you further, the material is presented in small, easy-to-digest chunks that are broken down using frequent sub-headings.

There are many photographs, illustrations and diagrams used to give you a visual way of remembering the work. Each photograph has a caption bringing your attention to the main point so the link with the information is unmistakable. There are also numerous learning features built into this book:

What you will learn in this section

At the beginning of each section, you will find a list of all the topics you will learn about in that section. Each topic is numbered, which is especially useful when you are revising, as it will be quicker to find relevant information and to check you know all the points you are supposed to.

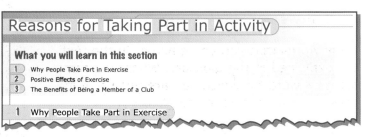

Tasks

Each section of work involves completing a series of numbered tasks. Completing tasks involves referring to the work just read or discussed in class. Tasks need to be recorded in your own book or file.

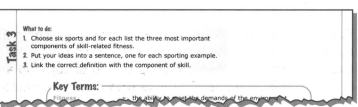

By keeping your book up-to-date and tasks complete, the work recorded will build up into your personal revision document. It is important that when you are working, information you write down can be read easily when you refer back to it. Take enough time to make your words legible.

Active Challenge

These are thought-provoking tasks, which often involve working with a partner. Completing these tasks will open your mind to the section being worked on and give you the chance to add verbally to the topic.

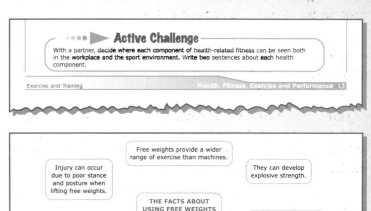

Using a spidergram

Spidergrams are quick and easy to complete. They are an excellent way of recording and remembering the main points of a section.

Key Terms

Wherever there are words in **bold** in the book they will be found in the key terms section. This indicates important words for you to remember together with their definitions.

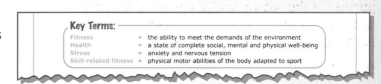

Summary

At the end of each section there is a paragraph that rounds up the essential information that you need to remember from the topics covered. It acts as a short collection of the ideas that are the most important to the section. When revising, the summaries can be used as a starting point to remind you of the main ideas. You can then add to them with more detailed information from memory or by re-reading the text.

Glossary

Many words that you come across in the text are explained in the glossary. When you come across a word for which you are unsure of its meaning – look it up in the glossary.

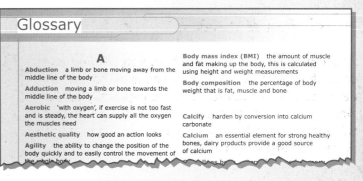

You and the exam

You could view the exam as a competition – a competition to get a better grade than pupils nationwide who have chosen to take this exam. So give yourself the best chance. If you are absent it is up to you to copy up any work missed. Gaps in work are gaps in knowledge. Students who have completed all of the work give themselves the best chance of success.

What you will learn about in this section

1. Why People Take Part in Exercise
2. Positive Effects of Exercise
3. The Benefits of Being a Member of a Club

1 Why People Take Part in Exercise

There are many reasons for taking part in sport. A person will choose a type of activity according to the benefits they want from physical exercise. A person who chooses exercise may do so solely because they enjoy the activity, but other positive changes may result as well. General health (both physical and mental) and social behaviour (how people mix with others and make friends) may improve, whether planned for or not. In some cases people can gain employment in an area linked with their sporting interests.

Owing to the wide range of rewards from exercise, most people can benefit whether the activity is strenuous or not. It is the health and fitness rewards that make exercising special in comparison with other leisure pursuits.

encourages friendships · enhance body shape · gives opportunity for competition · provides physical challenge · gain membership of a club · gives enjoyment · reduces stress-related illnesses · look good, feel good · **Reasons for taking part in exercise** · appreciate good performance · gives a new hobby · provides excitement · encourages co-operation · can increase life expectancy · allows us to take part in the sport · chance to mix with new people

▶ Active Challenge

Choose five reasons why you participate in sport and discuss them with a partner. Use the above diagram to help you decide your reasons.

Health

The general health of a person, both physically and mentally, may improve as a result of regular exercise. Not only may the heart and lungs become more efficient but success in sport can improve self-confidence which can influence other parts of life. Failure in sport can lead to disappointment or depression.

Physical effects of exercising

Fitness

Generally the more you exercise, the more your body is able to meet demands of exercise. Toning muscles can help posture. Exercising can increase strength, stamina, mobility and flexibility.

Enhance and change body shape

With regular exercise the muscles become toned: this is a tightening of the muscles in a state of readiness to work. Depending on the type of training programme, the shape and size of the muscles will begin to develop. Many people want greater **muscle definition**. Exercise at the correct level burns calories and, as long as the dietary intake remains the same, a person may lose weight with the extra activity.

Increase life expectancy

Regular exercise increases the efficiency of the heart, circulatory system and lungs. This also leads to an improvement in a person's general health. A person who has good general health can suffer less from minor ailments and may recover from serious illness more quickly due to the condition of their body.

Research carried out by the Department of Medicine at the University of Dundee came to the following conclusions: 'Older people with better health habits live healthier for longer' and 'Regular physical activity in old age can "rejuvenate" physical capacity by 10–15 years'.

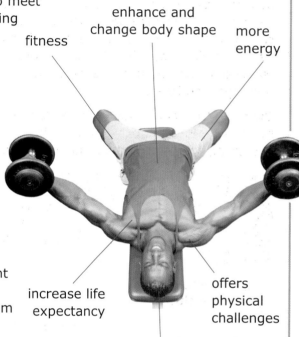

fitness

enhance and change body shape

more energy

increase life expectancy

offers physical challenges

reduces stress-related illnesses

More energy

When exercise is carried out regularly the body begins to respond to the activity. The body may become stronger, more enduring and more flexible. As a result, the body can work harder without becoming tired and breathless.

Reduces stress-related illnesses

When involved in physical activity the **stress** a person may feel is often forgotten for a time. This can have a positive effect on the functioning of the heart and so **stress-related illnesses** may be reduced.

Offers physical challenges

Whether taking part in a team sport or an individual training programme there will be targets to meet. Following a plan will help the performer to meet targets of physical self-improvement in skills, techniques, speed and strength.

Mental effects of exercising

look good, feel good

feeling of well-being

sets physical challenges

personal development

gives enjoyment

interest/hobby

reduces stress

excitement through the activity

opportunity to appreciate the activity

Look good, feel good

The improvement to general body shape and posture can result in people feeling more positive about themselves. They may also feel they have extra energy to do more things in life.

Feeling of well-being

An improvement in the efficiency of the body systems and body shape brought about by regular physical activity can give a person a sense of well-being.

Sets physical challenges

A person may take up physical activity later in life for the first time since school or be a regular exerciser. Whatever the circumstances, targets for development can be set so progress can be made. The satisfaction of reaching a higher standard through hard work, determination and effort can be what keeps a person continuing with exercise.

Personal development

Certain physical activities can present a person with challenging situations. By seeing problems through, whether individually or as a member of a team, and reaching the set goal, a person can develop courage and confidence.

Gives enjoyment

There are various reasons why a person enjoys an activity, it can be the physical challenge, the tactical battle to outwit the opponent or the fun of playing as a team to achieve success. There is a sport suitable for everyone and those who seek exercise can usually find a pursuit to satisfy them.

Interest/hobby

Starting a new interest can extend the knowledge of the individual. New tactics, skills, strategies and safety factors may have to be learned. As the skills develop, personal pride in the new achievement is felt and so pleasure and satisfaction result.

Reduces stress

Some activities are extremely competitive. These activities can act as a release valve for aggressive behaviour so that a person's general life is calmer. Having a hobby is something to look forward to and when taking part in a sport or activity a person deals with a new set of challenges; this can take their mind off problems of daily life.

Excitement through the activity

Some activities are attractive because they are exciting to perform. Skiing, climbing, skate-boarding and BMX track racing are all examples of sports that attract people because of the thrill and adrenalin rush they provide.

Opportunity to appreciate the activity

From taking part in an activity, a person will realise how difficult the skills are to perform. Using their knowledge of good technique, people can learn to appreciate others' skills and recognise good quality performance and the **aesthetic quality** of a move. A gymnast understands the degree of difficulty in a movement; a rugby player, seeing a player avoid several tackles in order to score, may appreciate the skills needed for this action more than a non-player.

Here the crowd are appreciating a sporting performance by Julian Knowle at Wimbledon in 2002. However, only those that have played a game can truly appreciate the skills involved.

Task

What to do:

1. Link each sentence below to a heading.
2. Make up your own sentence for each heading.

> Think about the positive effects of exercise. Perhaps link your ideas to sports and activities you are good at.

Headings

More energy   Increase in fitness   Feeling good   Life expectancy will increase
Appreciating the finer points of the activity   Excitement through the activity
Learning new skills   Meeting the challenges

Sentences

"Having played the game, I can see how good top-class sportspeople are."

"My pulse rate per minute is reducing; this means my heart is becoming more efficient."

"The rush of skiing my maximum speed downhill is what I really enjoy."

"Despite my training sessions getting harder, I am able to work for longer without tiring."

"I enjoy starting a new sport and learning and using the new skills involved."

"Through exercising regularly I have lost weight; this makes me feel positive about myself."

"I am becoming more confident about my ability to meet the challenges of the sport and realise how important it is to keep to my plan."

"I exercise for general fitness so I can keep my heart and lungs working in good order for longer."

3 The Benefits of Being a Member of a Club

A person attracted to sport may join a club so that they can participate in their chosen activity. They will not only improve physically but personal and social benefits may follow as well. As they improve their skills and abilities, a person's confidence may rise and so they feel ready to enter club competitions and compete against other clubs.

Encourages co-operation

In any club there are many jobs to complete for its overall success. The obvious one is to be a member of a team, but there are duties necessary for the general running of the club too. For example, fixtures need to be arranged, finances have to be looked after and the facilities have to be maintained. By working together for the good of the club, a person can be a player and an organiser or helper, co-operating with fellow members for maximum success.

Opportunity for competition

Many clubs arrange matches against other teams. This gives an opportunity for members to pit their skills against others in an effort to outplay and beat the opposition. The competitive approach needed in sport can link qualities needed in everyday life. In the relatively safe environment of sport, a competitive characteristic can develop that may help effectiveness at work.

Mixing socially with new people

Training with club mates and performing against other teams gives a person the opportunity to meet a large number of people. This can expand the variety of acquaintances a person has. Through these experiences a person can become more outgoing and confident in the company of others.

Some sports provide time during the game for socialising.

Encourages friendships

By being a member of a club, a person meets others with the same interests. After a club event there is usually a social drink and, by regularly attending such social events, friendships can form.

Allows us to take part in a particular sport

In some instances the only way to participate or compete in a sport is to be a member of a club. Clubs make taking part in an activity viable, as the equipment and coaching may be too costly otherwise.

What to do:

1. Write out what you would say to a friend to encourage and persuade them to join a sports club. Include at least four different reasons.

Key Terms:

Aesthetic quality	► how good an action looks
Muscle definition	► muscle shape
Stress	► anxiety and nervous tension
Stress-related illnesses	► these include heart attack, ulcer, high blood pressure

Summary

There are many advantages of taking part in physical activity. A person in the habit of regular exercise could benefit from their healthy lifestyle. Physically, the body and its systems can increase in fitness, and be able to meet the demands of their environment and the added demands of the activity. A stronger body may increase life expectancy.

Personal development can come about through the challenges of exercise. A person may develop determination, courage and a positive attitude as a result of taking exercise; in turn this may spill over into general life and positively affect a person's attitudes. As a member of a group, club or team, co-operation, teamwork and friendships may develop as well.

Task 2

Health, Fitness, Exercise and Performance

What you will learn about in this section

1. The Definition and Components of Health
2. Individual Exercise Needs
3. Different Exercises for Specific Activities
4. The Definition and Components of Fitness
5. About Performance
6. Health-related Exercise and the Effect on Skills

1 The Definition and Components of Health

The World Health Organization (WHO) gives a complete definition of what it considers **health** to be:

'a state of complete mental, physical and social well-being, not simply the absence of disease or infirmity'.

Mental health can be regarded as the ability to concentrate on a subject for a long period of time, control emotions and think logically through a problem. This could be achieved by regularly meeting people that you take part in activities with. In a sports context this could be as a member of a club, gym or society.

To achieve physical well-being, a performer would concentrate on five areas of health-related exercise (HRE). One model might be to follow a programme of exercise conforming to the minimum level of **fitness** required, which would improve the condition of the cardiovascular system.

Cardiovascular fitness relies on a healthy heart, blood and blood vessels. How active a lifestyle a person can lead depends on the condition of these.

Muscular endurance is the ability of the muscles to move weight over a long period without tiring and losing effectiveness.

Components of HRE

Flexibility is movement at a joint to its fullest range. With regular practice the joints can get nearer to their maximum range of movement.

Muscular strength can be seen in a person who can lift heavy weights. Strength is defined as the ability to lift a maximum weight in one attempt.

Body composition is how the body is made up in terms of bone, muscle and fat. The percentage of fat and muscle can be changed according to diet and exercise. Bone structure gives us our build.

2 Individual Exercise Needs

Maintaining the condition of the components of health, at a level at which people can carry out their everyday working lives without excessive fatigue, is essential. The effort required to get these components into a good condition will vary according to the individual. Each person has their own natural fitness level and so everyone has different requirements to maintain their minimum level of fitness.

Each type of work demands a certain level and type of fitness. Sedentary jobs, those where little physical effort is exerted, like working in an office, need a lower fitness level than manual jobs, like working for a removals firm. Yet, each active job differs as the type of fitness required by a removal person is different to that needed by a postal worker, for example.

High intensity effort requires muscular strength.

Sedentary work only requires low fitness levels.

Working moderately over long periods needs endurance qualities.

3 Different Exercises for Specific Activities

Just as each job has a different demand on fitness levels, so too do the various sporting activities. Some activities depend on the development of only a few health components, others need a combination of all of them.

To exercise effectively for any length of time, without tiring or becoming less efficient, requires the training of the cardiorespiratory system. The better the heart and lungs work, the greater is the efficiency of the body getting oxygen to the working muscles and removing waste products from the body.

The development of muscular endurance requires light to moderate exercise over long periods, whereas developing muscular strength needs short bursts of maximal effort. To execute actions with the correct technique and least likelihood of injury relies on the joints having good flexibility and muscles that can control the movement of these joints safely.

Body composition plays an important part in the effectiveness of the performer. There is an ideal body shape for each activity (somatotype is explained in detail on page 55). Athletes can improve their shape:

- by controlling their diet and choosing the correct combinations of food
- by eating the right amounts of food
- by the amount of exercise completed.

 **Active Challenge**

With a partner, decide where each component of health-related fitness can be seen both in the workplace and in the sport environment. Write two sentences about each health component.

4 The Definition and Components of Fitness

Fitness is different from health. A definition of fitness is:

'the ability to meet the demands of the environment'.

Having the minimum level of fitness will allow a person to go about their everyday lives and meet its demands without tiring. Fitness, therefore, is concerned with the physical condition of a person. Walking to the bus stop and completing tasks at work are both actions that should be completed without exhaustion. Each person has a different set of physical demands in their day, so each person's minimum level of fitness differs. If a person does not exercise and does not keep each of the components of HRE in good condition then daily tasks will become more difficult to complete.

The idea of various levels of fitness applies to different sports too. To take part in any sport requires a combination of fitness and performance. Exercise is a series of physical activities that improve health and physical fitness. A person may be fit to play badminton, but not fit in the necessary way for tennis. Each activity has its own set of requirements that the player must meet in order to succeed. The exercises, therefore, for each activity's training session will be different in order to fit with the requirements of the sport. By choosing and working on the most appropriate exercises the performance will improve.

5 About Performance

Performance is 'how well a task is completed'. This may be judged on whether the skills are performed with correct technique or whether the action, irrespective of technique, resulted in success. Often players who have good technical ability are successful. Top-class sportspeople spend much time perfecting their technique in order to compete successfully at the highest level.

The correct technique is how physically accurate the body matches the acceptable way of performing a skill. Although each performer will have a slightly different action depending on their height and build, good technique involves:

- good body shape at preparation, moment of contact and follow-through phases
- balance of the body
- speed of execution.

Identify the differences in hurdling technique between the school pupil and Colin Jackson.

What to do:

1. Look at the pictures above and spot the points of good technique. Write a sentence on each of them.

Example: Colin Jackson's body is square to the lane, maintaining the running action as much as possible.

Task 1

The condition of the five components of health has a great effect on the amount and quality of exercise, training and performance a person can achieve.

Cardiovascular fitness

Ice skaters need good cardiovascular fitness.

The good condition of the cardiovascular system allows for efficient transportation of blood to the necessary parts of the body in order that the body can meet the extra demands of exercise.

In training, if the cardiovascular system is not fit then the ability to keep working is reduced and so the required skill level is less likely to be reached. In competition, fatigue and breathlessness would prevent a person playing to the required standard or even continuing the activity in some instances.

Muscular strength

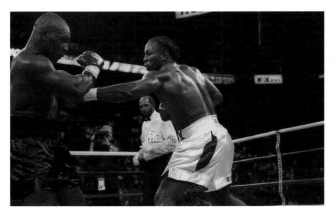

Lennox Lewis uses his muscular strength to overpower Mike Tyson.

Muscular strength, in itself, can be used to over-power an opponent. A player who can combine strength with speed can create power, which is especially useful when playing a forehand drive down the line in tennis, in order to pass an opponent at the net, for instance.

Having poor strength may prevent a player shooting with the required amount of power to beat a goalkeeper. In contact sports, like judo, a weak player gives little resistance to an opponent with muscular strength.

Muscular endurance

Good muscular endurance prevents the body tiring quickly.

Muscular endurance is essential for long-distance events such as 10 000m racing. The body is able to keep working for a long time without tiring and so has more chance of winning.

Flexibility

Controlled use of the full range of movement available at a joint can allow for the execution of the correct technique, improving performance and lessening the risk of injury. Where resistance to a force is necessary, the muscles must be strong enough to prevent over-extension beyond the fullest range. For example, players in a rugby scrum must have muscles strong enough to prevent over-extension of their shoulders.

Romanian, Dana Carteleanu, demonstrates her flexibility.

Body composition

Success in sport can depend on choosing the most appropriate sport for your build. The amounts of fat, muscle and bone in the body will change the shape of a person making them more or less suitable for a particular activity. A particular sized skeletal frame may lend itself to a certain sport or position in the team. The longer the bones making the frame, the taller a person is; this would be advantageous to a basketball player or goal shooter in netball. Shorter bones make for a smaller frame, suiting the needs of a jockey, for example.

Most jockeys have a small skeletal frame and a minimal fat component.

A person's frame size is an important part of their body composition. To determine your frame size, measure the circumference of the smallest part of your wrist. Use the table below to determine your frame size.

Determining frame size based on average height using wrist circumference

Frame	Men	Women
small	less than 165 mm	less than 152 mm
medium	165–191mm	152–159 mm
large	more than 191 mm	more than 159 mm

Body fat

Retired sumo wrestling champion, Konishiki, weighed over 275kg.

Extra weight is good for some sports. A member of a tug-of-war team or a prop forward in rugby usually has a high level of fat proportion, but this is usually combined with strength in order to make the person efficient in the activity.

Having extra weight can make a person slow and unable to keep working at a moderate to hard level for long periods. This is because the extra oxygen needed to keep the muscles working cannot be supplied at the pace needed by the cardiorespiratory systems (heart and lungs). As a result, fatigue sets in, injury is more likely and so the activity has to stop.

What to do:

1. Describe the positive effects in sport of having well-developed HRE components.

2. Describe the negative effects in sport of not having well-developed HRE components.

Write your answers in sentences and give an answer for each of the components of HRE.

> Use the examples previously given as guides, but try to think of your own.

Task 2

Skill-related Fitness

What you will learn about in this section

1. Definition of Skill-related Fitness Components

1 Definition of Skill-related Fitness Components

Balance – the ability to keep the body stable whether still, moving or in a different shape by keeping the centre of gravity over the base.

Reaction time – the time it takes to respond to a stimulus.

Speed – the fastest rate at which a person can complete a task or cover a distance.

COMPONENTS OF FITNESS

Agility – the ability to change direction quickly and still keep control of the whole body.

Power – the ability to apply a combination of strength and speed in an action.

Co-ordination – the ability to use two or more parts of the body at the same time.

Most sports have a combination of all the components of skill-related fitness. Each sport has its own special mix of skill-related fitness components to master in order for a player to be successful. Some sports need more power and strength, like throwing events in athletics, whereas others, like badminton, need agility and co-ordination.

The examples below show three different sports each requiring different components of skill-related fitness.

Australia's Alison Peek playing hockey.

Track cycling.

Denise Lewis throwing a javelin.

What to do:

1. Choose six sports and, for each, list the three most important components of skill-related fitness.
2. Put your ideas into sentences, one for each sporting example.
3. Link the correct definition with the component of skill.

Key Terms:

Fitness	► the ability to meet the demands of the environment
Health	► a state of complete social, mental and physical well-being
Skill-related fitness	► physical motor abilities of the body adapted to specific sports

Summary

A healthy person has a good balance of mental, social and physical well-being. Fitness relates to the physical attributes of the person and how well they adapt to the demands of the environment in which they function. These surroundings can be their everyday environment or in connection with sport.

The components of skill-related fitness are associated with sport. These identify certain abilities that are directly related to sporting situations. The more accomplished a person is at these components, coupled with their ability to adapt them to the intensity of competition, the more likely it is that success will follow. Each different sport requires the development of a certain combination of these areas for success.

The development of the components of health-related exercise have a direct effect on a player's ability to complete the skills successfully and so achieve favourable results.

Principles of Training

What you will learn about in this section

1. What Are Principles of Training?
2. How the Principles Help the Performer
3. Details of the Principles
4. What is a Personal Exercise Programme?
5. Link the PEP with the Effects of Exercise
6. Preparation For Testing and Measuring
7. Types of Tests for a PEP
8. Types of Muscular Contraction

1 What Are Principles of Training?

The **principles of training** are the rules to follow when using physical activity programmes.

2 How the Principles Help the Performer

Each person has a different reason for exercising. It may be for leisure, competition, professional or personal pride. A person trains to improve performance. When the principles are applied, improvements in cardio, vascular and respiratory condition; fitness, strength, endurance and skill might be expected.

Each of the principles shows the way in which the body is affected by the degree and type of exercise undertaken. If these basic rules are to be adhered to, each stage should be followed and planned carefully. As everyone's fitness level differs, **systematic training** must take into account the **individual needs** of the performer. An understanding of body systems is vital: knowing the existing capabilities of the heart, lungs and muscles sets the degree of difficulty of the training plan. For training to succeed, the degree of difficulty or intensity is set at a personal level. Setting the demands and intensity of the exercise at the right level ensures it is safe for the performer. If the demands are set too low there will be no improvement; if too high injuries might occur.

Top-class athletes have a final competition in mind. The training process is systematically planned so they reach a peak of performance to coincide with that event.

What to do:

1. Write down a definition of the principles of training.
2. Write down the reasons why training principles are important to the performer.
3. What considerations should be made when creating a training schedule?

3 Details of the Principles

There are several principles, each influencing the training of the performer in a different way. Good training takes into consideration all of the principles and their effects on the body. They are essential to the planning of a systematic training programme so that an individual can improve their fitness. The main principles are specificity, overload, progression and reversibility. The **FITT** (frequency, intensity, time and type) components are other significant principles affecting fitness development.

Specificity

This principle requires an understanding of the needs of the game or event, for example, a goalkeeper will include lots of reaction work in their training. When applying this principle the activity is usually practised at the pace required in the sport. If a person trains too slowly then their skills will only be reproduced at the slower pace and the action will be unable to match the requirements of the game. At a school practice for your team, if you repeat the skills slowly then when you get to the game the other team may be quicker than you are. So, speed up your practices!

The actions in training should copy the actions used in the game. If a person needs good leg strength simply making them strong may not be enough. A cyclist will train their legs, whilst cycling, in a different way from a long distance runner, both need muscular endurance but the method of training is different. In order to become a better swimmer a person needs to spend most of their time in the water!

Overload

Muscle strength can be improved by making the muscles work harder than normal. Putting greater demands on the body by exercising can improve fitness. The point where exercise is demanding enough to have an effect on the body is called the 'threshold of training'.

Whether a person is training for muscular endurance or muscular strength, their aim is to train between 60–80% of their maximum.

The cardiovascular system works to take up oxygen so that the body can function. The total amount of oxygen needed is called the 'oxygen uptake' and can also be called the 'VO_2'. As the intensity of the exercise increases there is a greater demand for more oxygen to produce energy. Although there is more demand, there is a limit to the amount of oxygen uptake and this is called the **'VO_2 maximum'** (or 'max'). A simple indicator of when a person reaches a level between 60–80% of their maximum work rate is that they will be unable to talk to another person, as they will have too little breath to do so.

Muscular endurance is the ability of the muscles to keep working for long periods without tiring or losing quality of movement. By gradually increasing the time the muscles are required to work, they will improve their endurance capabilities.

For older people the threshold of training decreases. Working at 50% of their maximum heart rate will often have a positive effect on their cardiovascular fitness.

Progression

Exercising at the same degree of difficulty all the time will only maintain current fitness levels. As training starts to change your body tolerances, the same session will not have the same effect. Your body needs to be put under slightly more pressure to continue to improve. This is the idea behind the principle of progression. The need to increase the amount of difficulty of exercise gradually is reflected by the ease with which you complete tasks. For cardiovascular fitness the same amount of exercise will not bring your pulse rate into the **target zone**. After about five to six weeks there may be a need to change the programme. The resting heart rate also indicates improvement as it decreases, the fitter a person becomes.

Reversibility

Just as the body will increase in strength, tone and skill with exercise, it will lose them without it. The body needs to be stressed to maintain and increase strength. After an injury or illness, an athlete may have lost their strength and skill. Although a person can quickly improve their endurance capability, it can be lost three times faster than it can be gained. Remember, if you don't use it you lose it!

There is a combination of four targets (frequency, intensity, time and type) that need to be achieved to meet the **minimum level of fitness**. Training is adapted by changing any one or more of the FITT combinations.

Frequency

Frequency is the number of times exercise is undertaken per week. The more times a person exercises the more often their body is put under stress. Three or more times a week is the recommended number of times extra exercise should be repeated, to reach the minimum level of fitness. Top-class sportspeople have to train a lot more frequently than this if they are to achieve results good enough for their aspirations.

Monday 6–7pm

But remember that the body also needs time to recover from training. Training very hard, every day, may be harmful even for a top-class athlete.

Intensity

This is the level of difficulty of the exercise. For instance, when considering cardiovascular fitness your pulse rate can show you how intensely you are working.

Working in a target zone of 60–80% of the maximum heart rate is the level where fitness will usually increase. When training for strength the intensity is calculated in the same way. A person trains within the target zone, by finding the maximum weight they can lift and working to 60–80% of that weight. As the amount of weight lifted increases with training this adds to the intensity.

Wednesday 7–8pm

The pulse increase, when training in the target zone, of a 16 year old

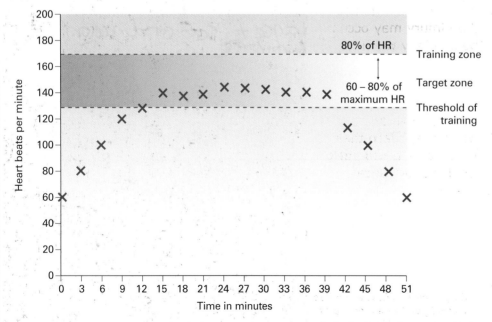

Friday 8–9am

Time

Keeping your pulse at 60–80% of its maximum for 20 minutes is the target. Warming-up is not included in the 20 minutes. The time begins when the pulse is at 60% target.

Type

This refers to the kind of exercise. It can be a matter of personal preference to suit the individual, if general fitness is the aim. If training for a specific event, then less of a choice can be made, as the training should reflect the activity. In this instance, type links closely with the principle of specificity. As long as the activity lasts for 20 minutes whilst maintaining 60–80% of the maximum heart rate fitness will usually improve.

What to do:

1. Write three sentences for each of the principles.

> F for frequency
> I for intensity
> T for time
> T for type
> The initial letters make the word FITT, which is easy to remember.

After the warm-up, exercising regularly for 20 minutes to 60–80% of maximum heart rate will increase the body's fitness.

Regularity

To make the body work harder than the minimum level of fitness, exercise can be repeated more regularly, made harder and last for longer. Training sessions can increase to five times a week. The intensity of the exercise can raise the pulse rate to 70% of maximum, instead of 60%. The duration of the exercise could be 30 minutes rather than 20 minutes.

By adapting the training programme in this way it more than doubles the FITT principles for the minimum level of fitness guideline (20 minutes, three times a week). Increasing training sessions in this way takes the athlete to a higher level of fitness.

Moderation

Reaching greater intensities of exercise is a gradual process. All athletes should find their balance between exercises. If they train too little then progress will not be made, if they train too much then injury may occur. Moderation is crucial. Changing the intensity will help to moderate training.

Peaking

The effects of the training will create peaks in an individual's performance. This is when they reach their best possible level of performance. Athletes try to peak at the time of the event. Loss of peak performance may result in poor form and bad results.

Sally Gunnell suffered an Achilles tendon injury. Injuries can occur at any time. A possible cause can be training too hard for an event.

Task 3

What to do:

1. Create a weekly timetable and plot a possible exercise plan.

> Remember to follow the FITT principles.

Round-up of ideas

All the principles are important when devising a training programme. The individual needs of the performer are taken into account and an exercise programme is set out solely for their capabilities.

When training for a specific event, specificity is a key principle. A swimmer will mainly swim, a runner will mainly run.

To gain from any training, overload must be applied. Muscles and body systems need to be subjected to stress. This is training more than usual above the threshold of training. The threshold is 60% of the maximum heart rate.

Once the performer is used to the exercise programme, then the principle of progression is applied. When applying progression the changes are planned systematically. This will make each change at the correct level and not injure the performer.

Applying the principles of FITT is vital to the success of the exercise programme. The regularity of exercising leads to improvements in fitness. Generally, the more frequent the exercise, the better the results that will follow. A person working towards more than the minimum level of fitness would train five times a week for 30 minutes at a time, with their pulse rate above 60% of its maximum. A serious sportsperson would need to ensure that their pulse was above 80% of its maximum when training for endurance. Moderating the number of training sessions strikes the balance between training too much – and causing overuse injury – and too little, when insufficient stress is put on the body to show progression. Once training has stopped then reversibility may occur. This is when the muscles **atrophy** – or weaken – due to lack of work.

Key Terms:

Atrophy	►	when muscles atrophy, they weaken and lose their strength and size because of lack of exercise
FITT	►	frequency, intensity, time and type
Individual needs	►	personal requirements for training
Minimum level of fitness	►	the resulting fitness level when someone exercises over a period of weeks, three sessions of 20 minutes, raising the heart rate to 60–80% of its maximum
Moderation	►	achieving a balance in training and not over-training
Principles of training	►	ideas behind effects of training
Regularity	►	repeating exercise sessions in a week to bring about improved fitness
Systematic training	►	planning a programme for an individual as a result of the effect of previous training
VO$_2$ max	►	amount of oxygen exhaled from the lungs after one maximum inhalation

4 What is a Personal Exercise Programme?

A personal exercise programme (**PEP**) is a series of exercises put together for a particular person. The exercise sessions follow all the guidelines of the principles of training to make them safe and suitable for the performer. To be effective, the PEP should be performed regularly and over a period of weeks. There will come a time when the programme is physically too easy to have an effect on the performer. This can happen about week 5 or 6 of the programme. At this stage, reviewing the programme is necessary. By applying the principles of training, the programme may be made more demanding.

5 Link the PEP with the Effects of Exercise

The diagram shows how the PEP develops. It always starts with **individual needs** and capabilities, moving on to the planning, performing and then to the reviewing. The review of the programme is most important if progress is to continue to be made. Re-testing the individual will show how their body has adapted to the programme. Increasing the FITT principle according to the results will ensure further progress.

Look at the individual and consider:

- test results
- cardio results (resting heart rate)
- respiratory results (**VO$_2$ max**)
- **body composition** (how much of the body is fat, muscle and bone?)
- which exercises they prefer?
- whether they like training on their own or in a group.

What is the purpose of the PEP?

- general health
- sport specific
- rehabilitation
- strength improvement
- flexibility
- muscular endurance.

Devising a PEP

Plan the programme, choosing from a variety of training methods:

- circuit
- weights
- continuous
- interval
- fartlek
- cross.

Review programme by applying the FITT principles of training:

- increase how many times individual trains – frequency
- increase the intensity
- increase time exercising
- vary the type of exercise.

What to do:

1. Using the ideas from 'Devising a PEP', write your own action plan of how a PEP should be organised.

6 Preparation for Testing and Measuring

To plan and prepare a programme of exercise for an individual, the clearest picture of their fitness level should be made. This is called a 'fitness profile'. This can be a general understanding of the heart rate and lung capacity or it can be made more detailed by testing aspects of skill. It is useful when assessing games players as they will need many different skills to play their game properly and the test can be designed to include these skills.

Why test?

- to have an idea of the next performance results
- to show weaknesses
- to show improvements
- to show how successful a training programme has been
- to motivate the performer.

How to evaluate

- choose the fitness component to measure
- choose a way of measuring it
- record the results
- work out what the results imply
- decide on the best exercises to do based on the results
- put the exercises into a training programme.

How to test

- each test should concentrate on one fitness component only
- the test should be easy to complete
- the performer should completely understand the test
- the test should be carried out in the same way every time.

 Active Challenge

With a partner discuss and decide on ten examples of sportspeople needing good leg strength.

1 Types of Tests for a PEP

Setting out a variety of physical tests helps to build up a person's fitness profile. The tests should relate to the reason for testing. There is little point in recording someone's cardiovascular endurance if the person is training for a throwing event in athletics. The first test will show the starting point of the athlete's abilities and fitness. After training, the next test will show the effectiveness of the training programme and point out changes for the future.

Below are a series of fitness areas in which an athlete may need to be trained. Each one has a test that measures the particular fitness component.

Cardiovascular endurance

Strong and efficient heart and lungs will help a player keep working hard throughout a game without losing breath and lowering performance. The bleep test can measure heart and lung efficiency reflecting the oxygen uptake (VO_2). The Harvard step test and the ten minute run are two other methods of measuring cardiovascular endurance.

Bleep test

How it works

- Athletes listen to the tape or CD.
- The athletes run to a cone and return only on the beep.
- If an athlete fails to reach the cone on the beep twice in a row, then they are out.
- The level they reached at that point is recorded as 'their level'.

Equipment needed

- 20m length course set out between cones
- 4 cones
- tape or CD of the test
- cassette or CD player
- recorder and recording sheet

CAUTION! These tests were originally designed for mature athletes; and are not suitable for all students. Serious injuries can occur if students push themselves too hard.

Bleep test results table		
Level	Shuttles	VO$_2$ max
4	9	25.5
5	9	32.9
6	10	36.4
7	10	39.9
8	10	43.3
9	11	46.8
10	11	50.2
11	12	53.7
12	12	57.1
13	13	74.4
14	13	64
15	13	67.5
16	14	70.9
17	14	74.4
18	15	77.9
19	15	81.3
20	15	84.8

Muscular strength

Muscular strength can vary in different parts of the body. The vertical jump test and the standing broad jump test measure leg strength. The pull-up test measures arm strength. Games players need to be able to jump for a ball in a challenge or to play a shot.

Vertical jump test

How it works

- Performer stands sideways to a wall.
- While standing with feet flat, performer reaches up with their arm nearest to the wall.
- The height where the stretched fingers reach is measured.
- Standing slightly away from the wall (for safety), the performer jumps vertically as high as possible using arms and legs for maximum height.
- They touch the wall at the highest point possible (by chalking the fingers a clear mark is left to measure).
- The distance between the two measures is recorded.
- The performer has three attempts.

Equipment needed

- indoor area
- measuring tape
- chalk
- recorder and recording sheet

Vertical jump test results table		
Rating	Male (cms)	Female (cms)
excellent	>70	>60
very good	61–70	51–60
above average	51–60	41–50
average	41–50	31–40
below average	31–40	21–30
poor	21–30	11–20
very poor	<21	<11

Muscular endurance

Strength endurance tests include sit-ups (like crunches), push-ups, chins and dips. There are other tests for different parts of the body. Performers, working for a lengthy period, need muscular endurance so they can keep their skill level high throughout the game.

Push-ups

How it works

- The performer adopts the front support position.
- Arms are extended, shoulder width apart.
- Partner places hand 10cm from the ground beneath chest.
- One repetition is when chest touches the hand, then arms fully extend.
- The activity is repeated as many times in a minute as possible.
- (When testing young people, the front support position can be adapted to kneeling.)

The push-up position. This can be adapted so that the performer kneels and performs push-ups from that position.

Sit-ups

How it works

- Performer lies on their back.
- Knees bent at a 90° angle.
- Feet flat on the floor.
- Partner has arm across performer's legs but is not holding their legs down.
- Performer's arms are crossed over their chest.
- One repetition is: curl trunk forward until hands touch partner's forearm and return.
- The activity is repeated as many times as possible in one minute.

Equipment needed

- indoor area
- mat for safety
- stop-watch
- recorder and recording sheet

Push-ups results table		
Rating	Male (18–25)	Female (18–25)
excellent	>50	>31
good	35–50	21–31
average	19–34	11–20
below average	4–18	0–10
poor	<4	

Sit-ups results table		
Rating	Male (18–25)	Female (18–25)
excellent	>49	>43
very good	44–49	37–43
above average	39–43	33–36
average	35–38	29–32
below average	31–34	25–28
poor	25–30	18–24
very poor	<25	<18

CAUTION! All results shown are for adults.

Flexibility

Players need to move the joints to their full range without hurting themselves. In football, tackling effectively needs flexibility. The sit and reach test is the most common test for flexibility.

Sit and reach

How it works

- Person sits, straight legged, with feet touching the start of the measuring block.
- They reach forward and place hands on the block to be measured.
- If they reach as far as their toes this measures 0cm, beyond their toes it is +0cm and if it is not as far as their toes it is -0cm.
- Recorder measures the distance along the block that the hands reach.

Equipment needed

- indoor area
- wooden block or bench
- measure

Sit and reach results table (cms)		
Rating	Male	Female
super	>+27	>+30
excellent	+17 to +27	+21 to +30
good	+6 to +16	+11 to +20
average	0 to +5	+1 to +10
fair	-8 to -1	-7 to 0
poor	-19 to -9	-14 to -8
very poor	<-19	<-14

A person performing the sit and reach test.

Possible results sheet

Names	Cardiovascular endurance Bleep test	Muscular strength Vertical jump	Muscular endurance Sit-ups	Muscular endurance Push-ups	Flexibility Sit and reach

What to do:

1. Round up the ideas of testing the components of fitness.
   For each of the components of fitness link:
   a. a test measuring the component
   b. the name of the test
   c. what area of the body it is working
   d. the anatomical name for the area worked.

Isotonic muscular contractions

This type of contraction occurs whenever there is movement of the body. The ends of the muscles move closer to make the action. This is the most frequently used type of contraction in games play. As a muscle contracts (shortens and fattens), it causes concentric movement. When it relaxes to its first shape, it is an eccentric movement (lengthens and flattens). The eccentric action is the most efficient of the two types.

An easy way to remember the difference between concentric and eccentric is to think about using the stairs at home. When walking up stairs, it is a concentric contraction, as the muscles are shortening to step up. When walking down stairs, it is an eccentric contraction, as the leg has to lengthen and stretch to the next step down.

Working the muscles isotonically improves dynamic (moving) strength. This is especially good for games players. It develops cardiovascular and cardiorespiratory systems and increases power and endurance. As isotonic muscular contractions come about through movement, there may be a greater possibility of injury than with isometric muscular contractions.

Isotonic muscular contraction takes place whenever there is movement.

Isometric muscular contractions

This type of contraction takes place when the muscle length stays the same. It is used for stabilising parts of the body and holding the body steady so that movement can take place elsewhere. Isometric muscular contraction improves static strength. It is easy to perform and needs little or no equipment. However, it does not develop power or muscular endurance. The cardiovascular and cardiorespiratory systems are not improved. Few sports require this type of contraction alone.

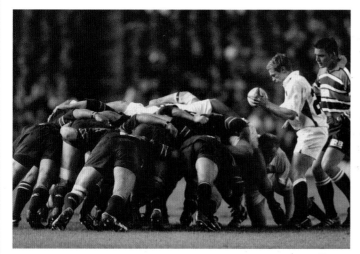 

Isometric muscular contraction takes place whenever the body is held still.

What to do:

1. Choose four sporting examples for each type of contraction.

Key Terms:

Body composition	▶ the amount of bone, muscle and fat making up the body
Isometric muscular contraction	▶ contraction with no movement
Isotonic muscular contraction	▶ contraction with movement
PEP	▶ personal exercise programme, training designed specifically for one individual
Target zone	▶ level of effort applied keeping within aerobic levels

Summary

People deciding to train need to think carefully about the type and intensity of the exercise they are to do. Age, ability, gender and experience will all influence the type of programme suitable. A clear awareness of the reason for training will influence the type of activities in the programme. The more serious the athlete, the greater intensity the exercise will be. Any part of the body exercised, if done so at the correct intensity, will develop. When increasing strength, the shape and size of the muscles change. It is important that an athlete develops the type of strength (isotonic or isometric) needed for the activity and exercises both sides of their body equally so that their shape stays as symmetrical as possible.

Methods of Training

What you will learn about in this section

You will learn about circuit training, weight training, interval training, fartlek training, continous training and cross training. For each method of training you will learn:

1. About the Training Method
2. What the Training Develops
3. How the Method Works
4. The Exercises Involved
5. How the Training Principles Apply

There are many training methods open to the performer. Each method works the body differently. The reason for training and the type of activity being trained for will steer a performer to a particular training method. When training over a long period, varying the methods used will reduce the risk of overuse injury and keep the athlete interested and fresh for each session.

1 About the Training Method: Circuit Training

Circuit training is a series of exercises completed for a certain amount of time after one another.

2 What the Training Develops

Circuit training can be useful in different ways. Depending on how the circuit is set up, it can develop power, strength, flexibility and endurance. At a basic level, it can improve the general fitness of the heart and lungs as long as the rests in between the activities are kept short. It can be adapted to incorporate skills for a particular game. Top-class performers, however, do not benefit much from circuit training as it does not allow them to achieve a high enough level of skill.

Circuit training can develop aerobic and anaerobic respiration. When using large muscle groups at each station (moving the whole body), aerobic respiration is in operation and this will develop the cardiovascular system. If exercising small muscle groups (such as the biceps and triceps) in turn at the stations, this is anaerobic respiration which builds strength.

3 How the Method Works

A circuit is made up of several activities. Each activity is given its own space in the gym or sports hall; this space is called a 'station'. Each activity is completed as many times as possible, these are called 'repetitions'. There is a set time for each activity, this is usually between 30 and 60 seconds. In this time as many repetitions of the activity are performed as possible. When all exercises at each station are completed, the circuit is finished. By repeating the circuit or adding exercises, the session increases in intensity. For general fitness the sequence of exercises works different muscle groups at each station. For beginners one circuit is usually enough.

4 The Exercises Involved

●●●●● ▶ **Active Challenge**

Cover the numbered list below without reading it. With a partner, study the picture. Try to name some of the exercises in the circuit. Make additions to the list of exercises from your own experience.

1. Step-ups
2. Skipping
3. Sit-ups
4. Benchlifts
5. Bench activities
6. Leg raises
7. Push-ups
8. Squats
9. Star jumps
10. Shuttle runs

Circuit training in school

5 How the Training Principles Apply

A circuit can be set for individual needs. Each person doing the circuit can have their own targets. This means that beginners and fitter people can work at the same time because they can work within the same time limits, but they each complete a different number of repetitions. Completing a circuit can be competitive and motivate people to work harder and achieve more repetitions. Even with inexpensive equipment, a successful general fitness circuit can be set up.

What to do:

1. List the advantages and disadvantages of circuit training.
2. Look at the circuit training picture. Change four exercises from general fitness to skills using a named sport.

> Choose skills from a sport. Are the skills repeated in the same way? Place them in the circuit.

Task 1

1 About the Training Method: Weight Training

The training involves shifting weight to increase the strength of muscles, using a programme of repetitions and sets.

Weight training machines are always set up and fully adjustable.

2 What the Training Develops

A person setting up a weight training programme needs to think about the following questions: What is the reason for doing the training? Is it for aerobic or anaerobic development? Which parts of the body are to be exercised? The answers to these questions will shape the whole programme.

Lifting heavy weights with few repetitions develops strength and power. This will build up strength, increase muscle size and use anaerobic respiration.

Lifting lighter weights many times develops muscular endurance. This way of adapting weight training can help a person who is rehabilitating after injury. By moving light weights, the muscles gradually get used to working and taking weight again in a safe and controlled way.

3 How the Method Works

Organising a weight training programme:

Assess – the performer's strength and fitness. Once the maximum a person can lift is known, the programme can start to develop.

Weights – light for aerobic and endurance, heavier for anaerobic, strength and size.

Number of exercises – the usual range is between 8 and 12.

Repetitions – complete 12–17 repetitions at 60–70% of maximum lifting ability for an anaerobic beginner. Use many repetitions for lighter, aerobic work.

Number of sets – a beginner might complete 1 set for anaerobic, building up to 2 sets after two weeks. More repetitions are completed for aerobic training.

Rest between sets – about 2 minutes.

Number of sessions per week – 3–4 sessions should show an improvement with up to 48 hours between each session.

Training to get the best results – speed of exercise: to lift and lower takes 2 seconds.

Safety factors – use of straps, adjustments to the seats, setting the correct weight and correct technique are essential for safe weight training.

Review – when the body has adapted to the stresses of the programme, changes are made. The strength of the performer is re-tested. If the programme has been set at the right level, the performer will have increased in strength.

New programme – changes are made to the programme. As a result, a combination of weights, repetitions and sets increases slightly.

Examples of weight training cards

% of maximum lift	Repetitions
60%	17
65%	14
70%	12
75%	10
80%	8
85%	6
90%	5
95%	3
100%	1

Good for beginners.

Complete 1 set of above (starting with easiest).

After 3 weeks, increase sets.

Weight training repetitions – the performer works through the order from 60%–100% in a session.

Lift 70% of max.

8 repetitions

3 sets completed

Good for novice.

Level of effort required means weights are lifted properly.

Little risk of injury.

Simple sets – the performer works at the same intensity throughout the session completing 3 sets of 8 repetitions.

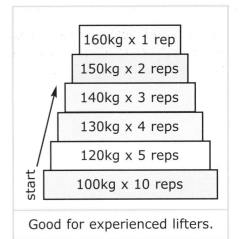

start

| 160kg x 1 rep |
| 150kg x 2 reps |
| 140kg x 3 reps |
| 130kg x 4 reps |
| 120kg x 5 reps |
| 100kg x 10 reps |

Good for experienced lifters.

Pyramid sets – the performer starts at the easiest weight working their way to heavy weights but with fewer repetitions.

4 The Exercises Involved (Two Ways of Training)

Machine weights

Using machines can be a safer way of weight training. They are technically designed to move in the correct way and are adjustable for different sizes of user. They are safe as they are steady and do not vary position apart from the designed range. This also has the effect of not training the stabilising muscles that may be needed for a sport. They usually have supports and belts to make sure the body is prepared in the correct position to shift the weight. They are always set up so are ready to use. Users starting a weight training programme find them easy to work. One drawback is that extra weights can not be added to the machines. This limits their use for the advanced performer.

seated leg extensions   hamstring curls   bicep curls

A variety of exercises in the gym

Free weights

Free weights can be used in a weight training programme. The use of such weights is specialised and needs lots of training so the performer works safely. Many top sportspeople use free weights. A person training with heavy weights must always use a spotter; this is a person who helps steady the performer and is ready to catch the bar or assist if the performer is struggling.

Injury can occur due to poor stance and posture when lifting free weights.

Free weights provide a wider range of exercise than machines.

More weight can easily be added to the lifting bar.

THE FACTS ABOUT USING FREE WEIGHTS

They can develop explosive strength.

When heavy weights are used, there is a need for a spotter in case the control of the weight is lost.

Skill is needed to lift the weights properly and without danger of injury, so beginners should not use them.

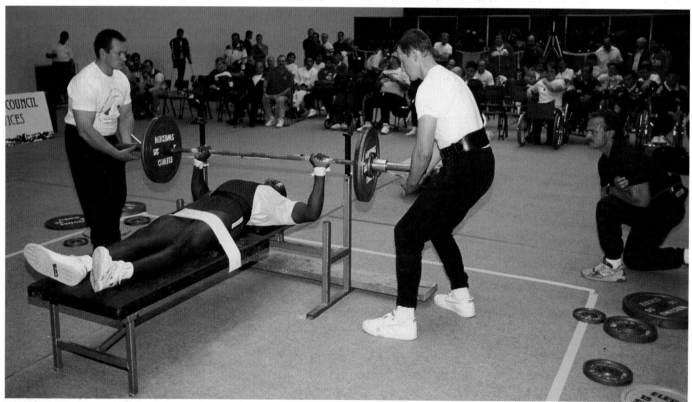

Spotters help make free weight training safe, as shown here at the British Disabled Powerlift Competition.

5 How the Training Principles Apply

With both types of weight training method, regular training improves the muscles' ability to move the weight. As the body adapts, the progression, overload and FITT principles are applied and the weights, repetitions and sets are gradually increased. This allows improvement of the muscles to continue. Lifting 60–80% of the maximum weight a person is able to lift will keep the performer within the target zone. Each session should last for no longer than 45 minutes.

A weight training card helps the performer to train safely and see progress

NAME	PERSONAL TRAINER		DATE PROGRAMME STARTED	
VISITS	1 2 3 4 5 6 7 8 9 10 11 12 13 14			
WARM-UP OPTIONS	JOG 5 MINS	CYCLE 5 MINS	EASY ROW 5 MINS	STEPPER 5 MINS
THEN	STRETCHES:	ARMS/SHOULDERS	LEGS/HIPS	ABDOMINALS
EXERCISE	STARTING POINT	PROGRESSION 1	PROGRESSION 2	PROGRESSION 3
TRICEP PULLDOWNS				
SQUATS				
HIP FLEXORS				
LATERAL PULLDOWN				
HAMSTRING CURLS				
HIP EXTENSORS				
BENCH PRESSES				
SEATED LEG EXTENSIONS				
COOL DOWN OPTIONS	WALK/JOG 5 MINS	EASY CYCLE 5 MINS	EASY ROW 5 MINS	
FINISH	WITH STRETCHES			

Task 2

What to do:

Answer these questions:

1. What makes each weight training session different?
2. How do free weight training sessions compare to machine weight training sessions?

> The training principles change the sessions: say how they do this. When comparing each type, think of the special features each method has.

1 About the Training Method: Interval Training

This method of training involves times of work followed by times of rest.

2 What the Training Develops

This method can be adapted to develop different types of fitness. Short bursts of pace, using anaerobic respiration, needed in games play, use short interval training. Prolonged moderate to hard pace, using aerobic respiration, needed in middle distance running events, uses long interval training.

Interval training is suited to individuals, working on their own, small groups of people and to larger numbers, like teams of players. Many sportspeople can benefit from interval training. The sessions can be adapted to practise the skills used in a particular game. Whether a runner, swimmer, footballer or netball player, interval training can be adapted to your sport.

The work is intensive and should be performed with accuracy and at competition pace. The times of rest allow performers to regain energy so they do not become too tired and can no longer carry on training. The times of work are repeated to form repetitions. Four or five repetitions make up a set. There may be four or five sets in a session.

An example of an interval training activity

Time limit for activity ⟶	Complete 4 sets of the following	Time limit for return ⟵
6–10 seconds	dribble and shoot ⟶	
	jog, return and rest ⟵	60–180 seconds
6–10 seconds	dribble and shoot ⟶	
	jog, return and rest ⟵	60–180 seconds
6–10 seconds	dribble and shoot ⟶	
	jog, return and rest ⟵	60–180 seconds
6–10 seconds	dribble and shoot ⟶	
	jog, return and rest ⟵	60–180 seconds

3 How the Method Works

Interval training can be adapted for different types of athlete and event. The working periods copy those in the event. The rest periods allow time for recovery in the same way that there would be quieter times during a game.

Long interval training

Work time is 15 seconds to 3 minutes. Games players and middle-distance athletes benefit from this type of training. The training copies the events in the need for bursts of maximal effort within the 15-second and 3-minute time spans. Even the best athletes cannot work at full pace for longer than 60-second periods so, when using this method, performers work at 80–85% of their maximum.

The resting times match the working times so the longer they work the longer they rest. The resting times are important to enable a performer to recover and continue the session. When working in larger groups it is more difficult for everyone to keep together due to the longer time limit and the variation in ability.

A 4-minute-mile runner could use interval training in the following way: repeat 10 x 60 second $\frac{1}{4}$ mile distances with 2 minutes rest between each run.

Short interval training

This training works on short bursts of maximal effort. The working times may be as short as 15 seconds. The performer aims to work all out for the whole of this time. Sprinters and racket sport players use this method to match the short bursts of maximal effort used in their events. A sprinter goes all out to reach the line as fast as possible and a squash player hits the ball with a burst of maximal effort. Due to the effects of the intensive effort on the body, rests of 2 minutes are necessary. In this time, the body has a chance to recover enough to carry on training.

4 The Exercises Involved

You will have used interval training in school already. Shuttle runs, dribbling relays, lay up shot drills and swimming 25m are all examples of exercises used for interval training. In a games or athletics lesson, you will have used shuttle runs. As you complete your shuttle run, that is one repetition. You rest while your teammates complete theirs. You may complete four repetitions before you are stopped; those make up a set. The teacher may give you another chance to complete the shuttle run after resting and so you will have then completed two sets.

Swimming, athletics and many games, such as football, use interval training. Here, Michael Owen practises his dribbling skills.

5   How the Training Principles Apply

As the periods of work and rest imitate the game, the principle of specificity is applied. To keep the performer improving when using interval training, the principle of progression is used. There are several ways to do this:

- the amount of recovery time may shorten and competitive pace work be increased
- the intensity or difficulty of the work may increase; this could be increasing the distance covered or amount of time run
- the number of repetitions or sets completed may increase.

What to do:

1. Choose and name a sport.
2. Design a 30-minute interval training session for that sport.

If designing a session for long interval training, include 5 repetitions and 4 sets. If using short interval training, use more repetitions and sets.

Task 3

1   About the Training Method: Fartlek Training

Fartlek is a Swedish word meaning 'speed play'. It involves exercise, often running, varying in time, distance and effort.

2   What the Training Develops

Due to the changes of intensity of the exercises, it trains both aerobic and anaerobic fitness. The athlete becomes increasingly capable of meeting the changes of pace in a competition or game.

3   How the Method Works

Speed, distances covered and the amount of time spent exercising change. In general, the session has work of varying intensity taking place over a minimum of a 20-minute period.

Fartlek can be an introduction to interval training and sometimes both can be combined to form a programme of exercise, owing to their similar content. This would suit a games player. The content of the session is flexible. The repetitions in the sessions, therefore, are made different to add interest to the training. Rest periods or less strenuous exercise give time to recover so training can continue.

0–15 minutes	*warm-up*
	sprint 10 seconds on flat
	jog on flat
	sprint 10 seconds uphill
	jog/walk downhill on flat
	run 150m on flat for 1 minute
	jog
15–35 minutes	*sprint 80m on flat*
	jog
	sprint 20m uphill
	jog downhill on flat
	sprint 10 seconds on flat
	jog/run downhill on flat
	sprint 10 seconds uphill
	jog/run downhill on flat
35–45 minutes	*cool down*

As an athlete's fitness improves the session will be planned to include increased intensity.

4 The Exercises Involved

Sprints, jogs and runs make up the session. These may have times set for them or may be for a certain distance. The session can be continuous with periods of intense work followed by easier work, which gives the body chance to recover. Sometimes the session can include periods of complete rest.

In Sweden, where this method originated, athletes use the surrounding hills and forests to train in. Many areas large enough to run in can be used to vary the training session such as in a park, at the beach and in the countryside. Fartlek training can be adapted to running, cycling and swimming.

5 How the Training Principles Apply

The principles of FITT adapt to keep the performer improving.

Heart rate of a 16 year old whilst fartlek training

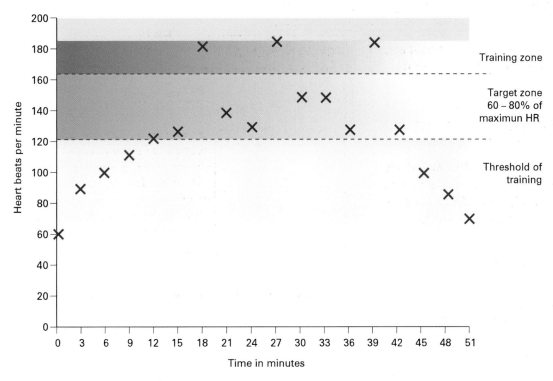

The heart rate rises and falls regularly in a fartlek session

What to do:

1. From your understanding of fartlek training, copy and complete the paragraph below.

   The word fartlek means _____ _____ in _____ where this training method originated. Athletes can use _____, _____, and _____ to run in. By using the natural changes in the countryside/beach the demands on the athletes _____. Uphill work increases the _____ of the exercise and the heart rate will rise. Sprinting to set markers trains _____. Periods of slower running help the athlete to _____ so that training can continue and the athlete uses _____ respiration.

1 About the Training Method: Continuous Training

This method exercises the body at a moderate rate, keeping the pulse at a constant level between 60–80% of maximum.

2 What the Training Develops

This training works the body aerobically and keeps the pulse at a high rate. Its effect is to improve the cardiovascular and respiratory systems. It can be adapted for both the health and fitness performer and the top athlete.

3 How the Method Works

After a gradual warm-up, the person training works their body at a moderate level throughout the session. The heart rate is above 60% of its maximum but below 80%. By keeping in this zone the work is aerobic and can carry on for a long time.

Continuous training suits a person who is training for the first time or returning to exercise after a period of non-activity, such as after injury. A person who specialises in long distance events can use this type of training out of season to maintain a good level of cardiorespiratory fitness. At the start of the season, continuous training can adapt as a gentle way to re-establish the cardiorespiratory levels. At this level, the work is moderate but can be adapted to be harder at a later time.

The use of a variety of machines, such as rowers, treadmlls and exercise cycles can adapt to continuous training.

4 The Exercises Involved

The types of activity that suit this training include cycling, swimming, exercise classes (aerobics), running and jogging. Many sports centres and gyms have specialised machines that adapt to continuous training. Treadmills, exercise cycles, rowing machines and steppers all lend themselves to this type of training. The activities are a good way of developing general fitness and can be adapted to suit both individuals and groups of people. If running is the exercise chosen, then it is inexpensive to start: changing the place of training is easily arranged, adding interest to the session.

5 How the Training Principles Apply

After several training sessions, the body will have adapted to the strains of the exercise. Checking the pulse rate during exercise will show if it is in the 60–80% zone, showing that the heart has become stronger as a result of the exercise. The speed of the exercise should be increased, in order to get the pulse rate into the target zone and continue to have an effect on the performer.

For the more advanced performer, greater stresses and demands are made on their body. By keeping in the training zone of 80–90% of their maximum heart rate and working for 15–20 minutes, the training will be effective. An endurance athlete, like a marathon runner, would use this method as part of their training programme.

Marathon runners use continous training within their training programme. Francis Naali of Tanzania won the men's marathon at the Commonwealth Games, 2002.

What to do:

1. Write six facts about continuous training.
2. How can the training method be adapted for beginners and more competitive performers?

> Think about: How hard does the body work? What effect does the exercise have on the heart? What types of activity can adapt to this method? Who would use this method of training?

Task 5

1 About the Training Method: Cross Training

This method combines different methods of training and has many advantages.

2 What the Training Develops

Each activity improves different muscle groups giving a wide range of development for the body.

3 How the Method Works

By changing the activity, parts of the body are able to rest and this prevents over-use injury. The variety of sessions can make training more interesting. Cross training can be adapted to suit individuals: a person may choose to run, play a game or do some aerobics work.

Cross training is best for developing general fitness, not necessarily training for top athletic results. This method allows individuals to work on their own or in a group. For those working in a group, as the activities change the groupings can change. This can widen the number of people a person knows as they train with a different group for each activity. Weather does not stop training as the sessions can be changed: an indoor session can be completed instead of an outdoor one.

Peter Marshall, a top British squash player, would follow a cross training programme as part of his training plan.

4 The Exercises Involved

Exercises for cross training include running, swimming, cycling, a chosen game and aerobics.

5 How the Training Principles Apply

Like the other methods of training, the FITT principles can be applied. As the performer adapts to the training, the sessions are gradually made harder, so that further progress can be made.

What to do:

1. Write three statements a person may make about the following training methods:

   a. fartlek training   b. continuous training   c. cross training

> You could use speech marks as though a person is actually saying the statements.

Key Terms:

Circuit training	▶ a series of exercises completed in order and for a certain time
Continuous training	▶ aerobic exercising, at a moderate to high level, with no rests
Cross training	▶ using different training methods in the same session
Fartlek training	▶ 'speed play', changing speed, distances and times of exercise in the same session
Interval training	▶ mixing periods of hard exercise with rest periods
Weight training	▶ progressively lifting heavier weights or lifting weights more often to improve strength; using light weights for an increasing length of time to improve stamina

Summary

The choice of the method of training can be a personal choice or it can be sport specific. Some methods suit certain kinds of event or game. People exercising for leisure can make any choice they want. People needing specialised training must choose the method that will improve their body systems and skills to the best of their ability. In this case, knowledge of the requirements of the sport is essential. By combining the knowledge of the sport and the abilities of the individual, an appropriate programme can be designed.

Individuals need their own programme of exercise as everyone is different and has their own reasons for training. Testing a person's capabilities first gives a clear idea of the level of training needed. By applying the FITT principles, both beginners and top athletes can be catered for. The key is to work the heart above the threshold of training. Working in the target zone will help general fitness; working in the training zone is for more serious athletes.

The principles of training create guidelines for improving the body. Plan progression carefully by reviewing the improvements made by the athlete. Systematically plan new programmes, increasing the intensity of the exercise when old levels have been adapted to. Remember, training at the correct levels will improve the body but it will reach a stable state from time to time and progress will stop temporarily.

Diet, Health and Hygiene (1)

What you will learn in this section

1. Seven Parts of a Balanced Diet
2. How Energy is Calculated
3. Individual Energy Requirements
4. Factors Affecting Energy Requirements
5. Special Diets for Sport
6. The Effects of Over and Under Eating
7. Individual Differences
8. Measuring the Body to Decide the Somatotype

1   Seven Parts of a Balanced Diet

The food we eat fuels our body just like petrol fuels a car. As the human body is more complex than a car engine, there are different types of food to keep the various parts of the body functioning properly. Food does the following:

- provides energy
- helps our bodies grow
- repairs injured tissue
- contributes to good general health.

It is important to have a balance of all of the seven types of food. Eating the correct quantities and combinations of food will keep the body systems functioning properly, keep hair and skin in good condition and reduce the chances of obesity.

In general, a **balanced diet** is important, but by changing the amounts of each nutrient eaten, a diet can be adapted to have a specific result for a sportsperson training for a particular event.

FOOD TYPES	ABOUT THE FOOD	AID TO THE SPORTSPERSON
Carbohydrates (sugars and starch)	Fruit, cakes, beer, sweets, granulated sugar and bread, pasta, rice and potatoes. Stored in the liver and muscles as glycogen. Converts to glucose and used as energy for muscles of the body, brain and other organs. Excess converted and stored as fat. Should provide over 47% of daily energy requirements and if training hard this should rise to 65–70%.	Provides a ready source of energy when the muscles require it. Carbohydrates in the highly processed form of sugars provide us with energy but no other nutrients so it is better to eat more starches. Athletes training hard use carbohydrates quickly, so diets should be high in this food type.
Proteins	Meat, fish, pulses (chick peas, lentils and beans), nuts, eggs and poultry. Builds body muscle, repairs tissue, enzymes and hormones. Proteins are broken down in the body as amino acids; 21 types are needed for our bodies to work properly. Our bodies can produce 13 types (non-essential amino acids) but the other 8 (essential amino acids) come from protein foods. Excess is converted and stored as fat.	Builds muscle and repairs tissue within the body. Essential after an injury to heal quickly. Sportspeople who need large muscle size need extra proteins.

FOOD TYPES	ABOUT THE FOOD	AID TO THE SPORTSPERSON
Fats 	Milk, cheese, butter, oils, chocolate, fatty meats, soya beans and corn. Provider of energy – recommended daily intake 30% of a combination of saturated, polyunsaturated and monounsaturated fatty acids. Can be stored in the body.	Increase size and weight of body. Important for performers who benefit from having extra bulk, shot putters for instance. Unnecessary weight can inhibit performance and lead to high cholesterol levels. Fats are a form of stored energy, released slowly when there is a lack of carbohydrates.
Vitamins 	Sources include fruit (vitamin C), liver and carrots (vitamin A), whole grains and nuts (vitamin B1) and vegetable oil (vitamin E). Help with the general health of vision, skin condition, forming of red blood cells and blood clotting, and the good condition of bones and teeth.	The general health of athletes is important if they are to perform well. When training hard, vitamins from the B group are used more and so need to be replenished. This can be done by eating more of that food type or using supplements.
Minerals 	Sources include, milk and saltwater fish (iodine), red meat, liver and green vegetables (iron), milk, cheese and cereals (calcium). Calcium helps growth of bones, iron helps the making of red blood cells and the way oxygen is carried in the body by the haemoglobin. The more a person exercises the greater the intake needed, provided by a varied diet or supplements. Excessive amounts of the mineral salt, can lead to high blood pressure.	Increase efficiency of carrying oxygen to the working muscles of the body. Iodine aids normal growth, essential for the athlete to help energy production. Iron helps produce red blood cells and so carry more oxygen round the body helping to prevent **fatigue**. Calcium helps blood to clot, aiding recovery from injury, and strengthens bones and muscles.
Fibre 	Leaves, seed cases, cereals and whole grains. Fibre, or roughage, helps digestion but contains no nutrients. There are two types: insoluble – this adds bulk to our food helping it to keep moving through the digestive system and so preventing constipation, and soluble – helps to reduce cholesterol, keeping the heart healthy.	Less cholesterol in the body makes the heart more efficient. By keeping the digestive system functioning regularly the body retains less waste.
Water	Fluids and food. Two-thirds of the body is made up of water. We need regular intakes to replenish what is lost in urine, sweat and condensation as we breathe.	Water allows the blood to flow more easily around the body. This is extremely important when exercising, as the body demands more oxygen, nutrients, heat control and waste removal. In endurance events, or when exercising in hot weather, water is lost quickly and can lead to dehydration and heatstroke if not replenished.

What to do:

1. What is the major role in human diet of
   a. carbohydrates?   b. proteins?   c. fats?   d. vitamins?
2. Give three examples of foods that are good sources of
   a. vitamins   b. carbohydrates   c. proteins.
3. What two types of carbohydrates are there and in what form are they stored in the body?
4. How does the sportsperson use the following:
   a. carbohydrates?   b. proteins?   c. water?   d. fats?

2   How Energy is Calculated

The body needs energy all the time, even when sleeping. This is because the body is still functioning – the heart is beating, blood is circulating, the body is breathing. This lowest form of energy requirement is called the **basal metabolic rate** (BMR).

Each food type has an energy value which can be calculated in two ways:

- Joules are calculated by a moving force = energy needed when 1 kilogram is moved by 1 metre by a force of 1 **newton**.
- Calories are calculated by a rise in temperature = amount of energy needed to raise temperature of 1 gram of water by $1°C$.

The main ways we understand the above calculations are as kilojoules (kj) and kilocalories (kcal). This is because diets and nutritional information on food packaging deal in large quantities and so the equation is multiplied by 1000 to make the figures more manageable. A food with a low kilojoule or kilocalorie value will have to be eaten in a larger quantity than one with a high value to do the same job.

3   Individual Energy Requirements

There are many factors that change the energy requirements of people. At different stages of life greater or lesser levels of energy are needed. Teenagers need more than adults. Women, on average, need less energy than men as they have a smaller build. As people get older their pace of life slows down and their energy requirements reduce. Even same age, same gender people rarely have the same energy needs owing to variations in their lifestyles and build. These factors are out of our control but what does dramatically change our energy requirements and is in our control is the amount of activity we undertake.

Below is an approximate calculation of the daily intake requirements for people of different ages.

Boys 15 years old	11 500kj (2700kcal approx)
Girls 15 years old	8800kj (2100kcal approx)
Adult men	10 500kj (2500kcal approx)
Adult women	8400kj (2000kcal approx)
Older men	8800kj (2100kcal approx)
Older women	8000kj (1900kcal approx)

 **Active Challenge**

Discuss with a partner the reasons why people have different energy requirements. Think of four different reasons.

4 Factors Affecting Energy Requirements

- Each sport has a different energy requirement.
- Length of activity.
- Intensity of activity.
- Level of opponent – easy game/lower level opponent.

Energy per hour needed for different activities

Activity	Approx. energy (kj)
Sleeping	252
Studying	420
Housework	798
Walking	840
Golf	1080
Gardening	1260
Cycling	1280
Swimming	1300
Volleyball	1440
Tennis	1740
Disco dancing	2100
Marathon running	4158

5 Special Diets for Sport

An increase in demands on the body from exercise means an increase in energy requirements. This should result in a change of diet to compensate for the new demand. The general diet for an athlete is high in carbohydrates, low in fat, with a high fluid intake, including **energy drinks** and/or water This provides energy and keeps the fluid levels balanced.

Diets can be organised around an exercise programme. This will involve timing when meals are taken, the content of the meal depending on the activity and the quantity of food to be eaten. A top-class athlete acquires knowledge of how to use the different types of food to their best advantage. Each sportperson's diet will vary due to individual differences of build, demands of the sport, position played in the team and any injury incurred.

Diet is important for athlete's at high levels of performance. It is seen to be so important that many sportspeople are guided by specialist dieticians and follow strict eating habits. The dietician will play their part in the performer's success just as does the coach. There are crucial times when a sportsperson can adapt their diet to help performance.

By adapting their diet over the following periods the athlete can get the best results:

- the week before the event
- the day of the event
- during the event
- after the event.

Carbohydrate loading

Traditionally, carbohydrate loading is linked with long distance events but other competitors can benefit too. Swimmers can use this diet effectively for their event. Carbohydrates are important to an athlete, as they are easy to digest and provide an instant source of energy. By eating more carbohydrates, a store of glycogen is built up in the body. In competition this store will reduce levels of fatigue and so help to maintain a standard of performance.

Diet for a long distance athlete

Pre-event

The week before an event a runner's training routine and diet change. Due to the excesses of previous training, carbohydrates are low in the body while proteins are high. This combination is not appropriate for a long distance athlete. So, four or five days before the race, many more carbohydrates are eaten in order to build up these energy stores for the event.

The training programme is now tapered so fewer miles are covered, allowing energy levels to build up and the speed of the shorter runs increases preparing for a burst of speed during the race. By taking in extra carbohydrates and fewer fats, together with reducing the intensity of the training programme, the body is able to store these nutrients, as glycogen, for use in the race.

The usefulness of carbohydrates is so widely recognised to the long distance athlete that 'pasta parties' are organised for the athletes the two days before the London Marathon. Eating foods such as noodles, rice, potatoes and even beans on toast will have a similar effect.

Day of event

On the day of the event athletes will choose, from preference and experience, either a large meal three to four hours before the race, or a lighter one up to two hours before the race. This is the final chance, before the competition, to make sure that carbohydrates are stocked up and fluid levels are high.

During event

The prolonged, moderate to hard intensity of a long distance race reduces the amount of water in the body. Low water levels reduce performance and prevent correct circulation and temperature control. Regular water intake is essential to the athlete to prevent dehydration (see page 96). Energy drinks help the body to work hard for longer by using the carbohydrates in them.

After event

An athlete must continue to drink fluids and energy drinks to replace the fluids and carbohydrates lost. High energy food can be eaten immediately after the race. Depending on the training programme following the event, a sensible meal including various carbohydrates is usual.

Taking fluids during an endurance event is essential.

What to do:
1. Make a ten-point list about carbohydrate loading and the procedure for food and fluid intake for a long distance event.

Include ideas on the week before, day of race, during race and after race.

High protein diet

This diet requires the intake of a large amount of protein. Weight lifters and athletes, needing a loss of weight over a fairly short period of weeks, can adopt this diet. High protein diets can also be used in a rehabilitation programme after injury for the repair of damaged tissue.

A body builder or a rugby player will use this type of diet to burn fat and increase muscle size. Taking creatine (a form of protein) supplements increases the effect. A rugby league player can eat as many as six meals a day taking in mainly proteins, some carbohydrates, but little or no fat. Throughout the day, they are encouraged to drink plenty of fluids and eat fruit as well as the prescribed meals. The protein will build up the muscle; carbohydrate will provide energy and fluids will keep the body hydrated.

Eating a high protein diet has the effect of reducing the storage of fat in the body. Some performers, who need to lose weight quite quickly, can use this type of diet. However, there is now evidence of long-term problems with this type of diet.

Problems with the diet

There are long-term effects of using high protein diets. When a body builder takes in a high level of animal proteins this raises the cholesterol levels in the body leading to a possibility of heart disease, diabetes, stroke and cancer. The performer using a high protein diet to control their weight can develop kidney damage in the long term.

6   The Effect of Over and Under Eating

How to lose weight – more exercise, less calorie intake.
How to gain weight – make calorie intake exceed energy expended.
How to maintain weight – balance calorie intake with energy used.

Changing their diet to make a weight or to keep slim can have major consequences on a sportsperson.

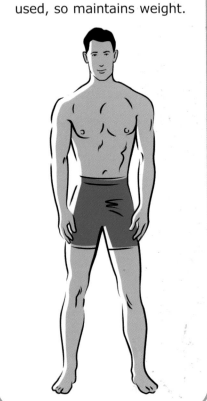

(Normal-sized person)
The amount of food eaten matches the amount of energy used, so maintains weight.

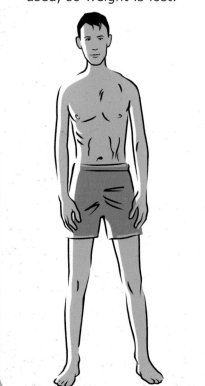

(Underweight person)
The amount of food eaten is not enough for the energy used, so weight is lost.

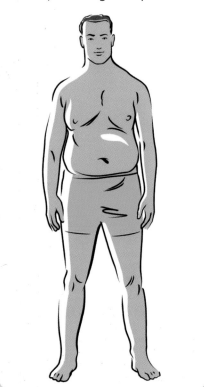

(Overweight person)
The amount of food eaten is too much for the energy used, so weight is put on.

Weight problems affecting performance

Each athlete has an **optimum weight** at which they perform at their best. This depends on the correct balance of height, gender, bone structure and muscle girth (measurement around the flexed muscle). Some athletes can keep to their optimum weight easily, whilst others constantly have to check what they eat. Some sports, like boxing and horse racing, demand a certain weight restriction; so for the boxer and the jockey, diets and quick weight loss are sometimes vital for them to compete. It is the fluids in the body that are lost when an athlete needs to make the weight category in a short period of time. The consequences of losing weight quickly can be that the body becomes dehydrated and the level of performance is reduced, making the competitor less effective. Some athletes will appear to be overweight but this is due to their large muscle girth and the appearance is misleading. If a sportsperson is overweight it can have a bad effect on their performance as well as a poor effect on their health.

The demands of some sports for an athlete to be the optimum weight are essential for the greatest success. The effect of having too much fat can restrict the flexibility of the joints and so the athlete cannot move appropriately to execute the correct technique. Carrying too much weight will decrease the speed of movement, slowing a player down in a game. A performer will tire quickly because of the extra effort needed to carry more weight. In some sports, like archery and bowls, where speed is not a necessity, then being overweight is not a problem. It may even make the person more stable and so help accuracy.

Height to weight chart for adult men and women

Are you the right weight for your height?

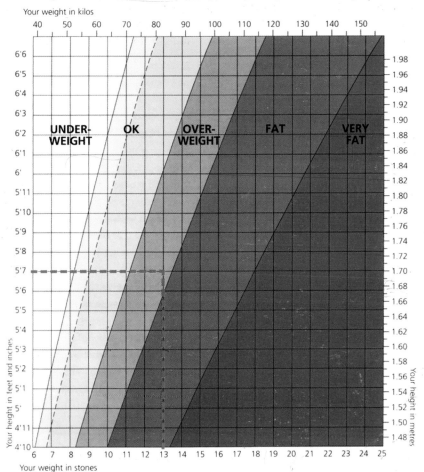

This chart is issued by the Food Standards Agency in the UK. The chart provides a guideline to adults showing what the correct weight of a person should be dependant on their height.

Degrees of being overweight

An **overweight** person can be said to be heavier than the average person of that gender, height and build. (See height to weight chart on the previous page.) The extra weight, however, is not necessarily a threat to the person's health (sometimes a lot of it is muscle).

Being **overfat** can have a direct effect on a person's health. In this category a person will have a high level of fat in comparison with their total body composition. Having this amount of fat can lead to obesity related disease: problems may include high blood pressure, stroke, cancer and heart attacks.

When a person reaches the stage of being **obese**, they are abnormally fat (more than 20% over the standard weight for their height). At this stage the health risks become more dangerous and can include diabetes, high blood pressure, heart disease, osteoarthritis and early mortality.

Being overweight is a problem of the twentieth century. Many nations now record more than 20% of their population as clinically obese and well over half the population as overweight. This trend has increased throughout the world as fast food chains reach various areas. In USA 60% of the population is overweight giving America the nickname 'the fat capital of the world'.

Possible dietary problems

In an effort to look like role models seen in the media, people put pressure on themselves about their weight, which can sometimes lead to eating disorders. Athletes may also do the same in an attempt to reach and maintain a low body weight ideal for their sport, but unnatural for themselves.

There are two main eating disorders:

Anorexia – a person does not eat, they see themselves as fat, the problem is the obsessive state of mind. This condition leads to excessive weight loss.

Bulimia – a person eats a lot and then forces themselves to vomit. This has the effect of weight loss.

Both eating disorders lead to bouts of depression and many severe medical problems, including kidney and liver damage, and even death.

Many people feel under pressure to become thin to look like their role models, this can lead to eating disorders.

Task 3

What to do:

1. Choose five different types of sportsperson.
2. Write a sentence on what they may say about their diet and how it affects them.

Include ideas on: energy needs of the activity, weight problems and how training changes natural food preferences.

There are many differences in people's physical shape and size.
The following are the main factors creating the individual shape of a person:

- height
- weight
- body fat
- muscle girth
- bone size.

Depending on the combination of these different components, a person may be influenced to participate in a certain sport or even to play in a particular position within a team due to the suitability of their shape and size.

Somatotypes

This is a method of identifying people by their body shape. WJ Sheldon devised this method in 1940; he originally adapted his findings to criminology. Professor Tanner studied sportspeople from the 1960 Olympic Games applied Sheldon's ideas to sport. There are three extreme categories of body type; each type is determined by the amount of fat, muscle and bone making up the body.

Identifying the three types

The three somatotypes are:

Endomorphic – tendency to put on fat, soft roundness of shape, short tapering limbs, small bones, wide hips.

Mesomorphic – high proportion of muscle, bone, large trunk, heavy chest, broad shoulders and narrow hips.

Ectomorphic – lean, fragile, delicate body, small bones, narrow at shoulders and hips.

Each type has a 1–7 score, 1 is low and 7 is high. Each person is measured to find their personal mark. A non-sportsperson may have the following combination 4, 3, 3, (4 – medium endomorphy), (3 – low mesomorphy), (3 – low ectomorphy).

Sport attracts extremes

There are very few people with the extreme examples of body type. Most people have a combination of all three. Sportspeople have more mesomorphic (muscle) and ectomorphic (thinness) than endomorphic (fatness) characteristics. A top-class sport, however, will attract the best extremes of body type suitable to that game. Basketball, for instance, will attract players who are all very tall and thin with sinewy muscles, falling into the ectomorph/mesomorph category.

Each sport is different and suits people of a certain somatotype.

What to do:

1. Put the following into the correct category for somatotype:

   a. basketball player   e. swimmer

   b. hockey player   f. marathon runner

   c. rugby player   g. shot putter.

   d. gymnast

2. For each of the above sportspeople write a sentence on how they might describe themselves.

> You may need to do some research to find out about the sports mentioned. Use your judgement to decide the somatotype by using the photographs above to help your decisions.

The three body types are the extremes; many people have a combination of different body types. When working out a person's type, their age, gender, height, weight, size of bones, amount of fat on the body and size of muscle are all taken into consideration.

Measuring somatotype is used to find the shape category of a person using size, composition and build. Knowing their somatotype can steer people into a sport to which they are naturally suited or show areas of the body that need to change in order to reach maximum success rate in an activity.

Fat ratio of the body

The fat layer is just below the top layer of skin on the body. Fat is a good insulator and can be of benefit in activities in cold climatic conditions. The amount of fat people have on the body varies with age and gender. Babies and women have thicker layers than men. Both sexes can increase their fat ratio as they get older. Men increase the amount around their middle; women the amount on their thighs and buttocks.

Measuring fat

A **skin-fold calliper** is an adjustable instrument that measures the amount of fat at different places on the body. The method is to place skin and underlying layers of fat between callipers, a dial gives the reading of the thickness of the flesh. There are four main measurements to take:

- Biceps – at the front of the upper arm
- Triceps – at the back of the upper arm
- Supra-iliac – at the front of the body above the hips
- Subscapula – at the bottom point of the scapula (shoulder blade).

In all cases take care not to include muscle in the callipers.

Skin-fold calliper being used to measure the amount of fat at the bicep area.

Measuring bones

Measuring bones gives the size of bones in relationship to the muscle and fat levels of the body. The places to measure are the elbow and knee joints.

For the elbow:

- Flex the biceps until the joint is at right angles.
- Use a condyle calliper to measure across the elbow at the widest point. This is a condyle measurement of the humerus.

Active Challenge

Using the same method as for measuring the elbow write how you would take the condyle measurement of the femur.

Measuring muscles

This measurement is taken, in centimetres, of a muscle while it is flexed and at its widest point. The muscles measured are the biceps (upper front arm) and gastrocnemius (back lower leg, commonly known as the calf muscle).

Taking a bicep girth reading:

- Hold the humerus horizontally.
- Flex the bicep so arm is at right angles.
- Take measurement around widest part in centimetres.

Taking a gastrocnemius girth reading:

- Stand with feet slightly apart.
- Flex gastrocnemius by standing on toes.
- Take measurement around widest part in centimetres.

People who regularly weight train increase the size of their muscles.

Active Challenge

Measure your partner's flexed bicep.

Key Terms:

Balanced diet	► daily intake of food containing right amounts and types of nutrients
Basal metabolic rate	► the level at which energy is used without exercise
Carbohydrate loading	► building up carbohydrates in the body to use in endurance events
Energy drinks	► fluids containing carbohydrates
Fatigue	► the body's inability to complete a task
Newton	► a unit of force
Obese	► a person who is extremely overweight (more than 20% over the standard weight for their height). This condition can lead to many health problems
Optimum weight	► ideal weight for a person, giving them the best chance of success in an activity
Overfat	► a person having more body fat than is recommended for their gender and height
Overweight	► a person carrying more weight than is recommended for their gender and height
Skin-fold calliper	► a device that measures the thickness of a fold of skin with its underlying layer of fat
Somatotype	► particular body type or shape of an individual

Summary

For general health, a balance of all seven nutrients in the daily diet is important.

Each food has a different energy value and use. A person who strikes a balance of food intake and energy output will maintain a constant weight. When an athlete understands the different qualities of food, they can use them to their best advantage and build special diets into the training programme. By eating certain foods in the correct quantities, athletes can change their natural shape (changing the fat ratio and muscle size), energy levels and recovery period, so helping them to be more effective in their sport.

Somatotype

This is the shape and body composition of an individual. The tissue ratio can be changed by adapting the type of diet consumed and exercise undertaken. However, extreme diets can badly affect the health of an individual. Certain somatotypes are better suited to some sports than others; shape may encourage a person to make a natural choice to take part in a particular activity.

Diet, Health and Hygiene (2)

What you will learn about in this section

1. Drugs in Society and Sport
2. Drugs and the Sportsperson
3. Performance-enhancing Drugs
4. Banned Method
5. Drugs Testing
6. Hygiene

1 Drugs in Society and Sport

Drugs are chemicals consumed, inhaled or injected into the body to artificially change its natural qualities. Some drugs are accepted in society, some have an age restraint on their use and others are illegal.

Each type of drug affects the body in a different way. Drugs can be used to develop the body in a desired way but they can also change the mental approach of a person. Some are addictive and people get into the habit of depending on them. When a body is manipulated in such an artificial way, there is usually a price to pay. Undesirable side effects may occur quickly but there may also be long-term health risks and possible shortening of life expectancy.

Socially acceptable drugs

Cigarettes

Cigarettes are a legal drug but are slowly becoming less socially acceptable. It has been recognised that smoking contributes to long-term illnesses (such as coronary heart disease).

When a person smokes, they take harmful chemicals into their body. The worst substance is tar, which collects in the lungs and is believed to be directly related to cancer. Tobacco contains nicotine, which is not a banned drug but some would say that it has an addictive quality. Nicotine affects the body by stimulating the brain to release noradrenaline, which is usually released in times of stress.

Smoking raises the pulse rate and so makes the heart work faster for no reason. The smoker's blood vessels contract, raising the blood pressure and

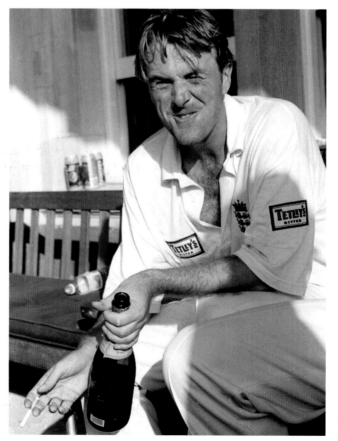

Bowler Phil Tufnell is shown smoking and drinking after the Ashes Test Match.

causing a sensation of cold. Smoke contains carbon monoxide and when this enters the blood stream it reduces the red blood cells' ability to transport oxygen. As a result, fitness levels are reduced.

In activities where the good condition of the cardiorespiratory systems is required, smoking is a major hindrance as it can affect the necessary blood flow around the body.

Alcohol

Alcohol is a socially acceptable drug but is banned in most sports as it has an unfair or detrimental effect on the performer. It can act as a sedative, slowing reactions and impairing judgement. It is dangerous if combined with a sport relying on judgement at speed, such as motor racing.

Socially unacceptable drugs

Drugs that are seen as socially unacceptable are those that are illegal to possess or use; there are many such drugs and they have various effects. A few are detailed below.

Cannabis

This drug is known as a depressant. It has the effect of making a person's reactions slower and their judgement poor. There is no use of this drug for the sportsperson.

Ecstasy

This drug is a stimulant. It increases a person's self-esteem, making them feel confident and good about themselves. It can cause slight hallucinations and after taking it a person will lose their ability to carry out regular tasks properly. It is of no use to the sportsperson as it affects a person's awareness, impairing their judgement.

LSD

This is classed as a hallucinogen. It affects a person's ability to make decisions as they see life in a bizarre way. It can cause flashbacks of strange experiences. It has no use to a sportsperson.

What to do:

Copy and complete the following sentences.

1. Smoking can affect the good _____ of the blood around the body and can cause _____ problems in later life. Cigarettes contain _____ which has an addictive quality.

2. Alcohol is a _____ _____ drug. In sufficient quantities it can _____ and combined with sport it can be dangerous.

3. Cannabis is a _____ and affects _____ as well as slowing people's reactions. These effects are of _____ _____ to the sportsperson.

4. Ecstasy is a _____, which can cause hallucinations. It stops a person _____ and is of no use to the sportsperson.

5. LSD is a hallucinogen affecting a _____ _____ and view of life. It is of no use to the _____.

2 Drugs and the Sportsperson

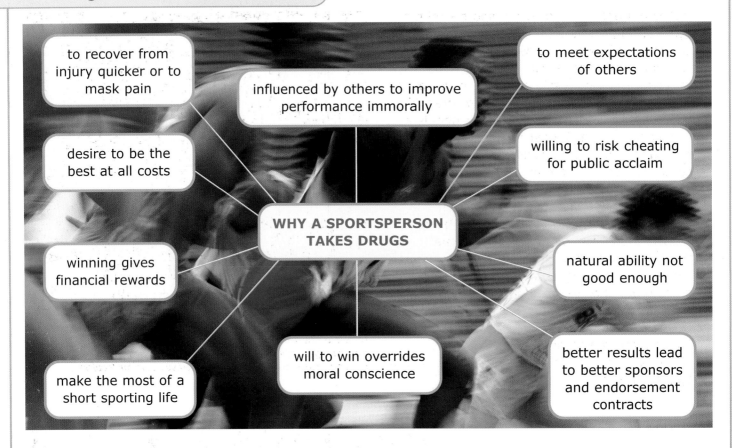

to recover from injury quicker or to mask pain

influenced by others to improve performance immorally

to meet expectations of others

desire to be the best at all costs

willing to risk cheating for public acclaim

WHY A SPORTSPERSON TAKES DRUGS

winning gives financial rewards

natural ability not good enough

will to win overrides moral conscience

better results lead to better sponsors and endorsement contracts

make the most of a short sporting life

3 Performance-enhancing Drugs

The rewards for winning can be great in sport. Some athletes are tempted to cheat in order to win. This undermines the integrity of the sport and so the governing bodies of different sports have clear drug testing policies to try to keep their sport 'clean'.

Each sport has its own list of banned substances, which are published to make it clear to performers and their coaches what cannot be taken during training and competition. The effects of taking performance-enhancing drugs are wide and varied; some help to hide pain, like methadone (an opioid analgesic) others develop the body artificially, like anabolic steroids.

The governing bodies work to try to keep a good name for sports and look after the interests of the athletes. The International Olympic Committee (IOC) medical commission works to: 'Protect the health of athletes ... ensure respect for both medical and sport ethics ... enforce equality for all competing athletes.'

IOC guide to classes of prohibited substances and methods of doping

Prohibited classes of substances:

A. stimulants
B. opioid analgesics
C. anabolic agents
D. diuretics
E. peptide hormones, mimetics and analogues.

Prohibited methods:

A. blood doping
B. pharmacological, chemical and physical manipulation.

Classes of drug subject to restriction:

A. alcohol
B. cannabinoids
C. local anaesthetics
D. corticosteroids
E. beta blockers.

Anabolic agents

- Most commonly used drugs in sport – mimic testosterone, a male hormone.
- **Examples of drug** Testosterone, nandrolone, stanozolol, boldenone, clenbuterol.
- **Effects** Increase muscle mass and develops bone growth, increase strength, allow the athlete to train harder. Has a quick effect so there is a rapid improvement. Increase aggression, so seen as good for competitive contact sports. Prevent muscle wastage and are an aid to rehabilitation.
- **Side effects** Has the greatest effect on women: deepens voice, increases facial hair, users have irregular periods and can become infertile. Men grow breasts, can become impotent and develop kidney problems. Mood swings, anxiety, aggression, face can swell up, high blood pressure, heart attacks, strokes. Increased risk of muscle injury and liver disease.
- Injected into the blood stream.
- Recent research indicates long-term users show signs of addiction.

CJ Hunter, the 1999 world shot put champion, served a two-year ban after testing positive for nandrolone on four separate occasions. He registered close to record levels, 1000 times above the legal limit.

Stimulants

- Second most commonly used drugs.
- **Examples of drug** Amphetamines, ephedrine, cocaine, caffeine.
- **Effects** Reduces feelings of tiredness so a person can train for longer, stimulates the central nervous system (CNS) and makes people more alert.
- **Side effects** User is irritable, unable to sleep, has high blood pressure, irregular heart beat, faster heartbeat.
- Some are addictive – amphetamines.

Stimulants improve reaction time.

Opioid analgesics (including narcotic analgesics)

- **Examples of drug** Heroin, methadone, pethidine, morphine, codeine.
- **Effects** Reduces the sensation of the CNS. Helps pain relief, so athlete is back from injury sooner, hides the pain.
- **Side effects** Loss of concentration, loss of balance, loss of co-ordination making sport dangerous. Using these drugs can make an injury worse and may cause a long-term problem related to the first injury.
- Usually, injected into the blood stream.
- They are addictive.

Diuretics

- **Examples of drug** Furosemide, triamterene, chlortalidone. Mannitol is prohibited if intravenously injected.
- **Effects** Speeds up work of kidneys by producing more urine. Reduces fluid retention, which causes rapid weight loss; used in sports where there are weight categories. Sportspeople use diuretics to 'make the weight'.
- **Side effects** Dehydration and possibly dizziness, muscle cramps, headaches, nausea, fatigue. Kidney illness can develop.

Peptide hormones, mimetics, analogues

- **Examples of drug** Human growth hormone (hGH), erythropoietin (EPO) synthetic substance that copies natural hormones of the body.
- **Effects** hGH develops muscle, makes the body use fat and helps reduce tiredness. Recovery from injury and training is quicker, increases red blood cells and so helps the endurance athlete.
- **Side effects** EPO thickens the blood inhibiting circulation, which can lead to a heart attack or stroke and hGH acts like anabolic steroids.

Naseem Hamed trains hard to make the weight, whereas a few athletes are tempted to use drugs.

Beta blockers

- **Examples of drug** Atenolol, nodolol. Some beta blockers are available on prescription to treat angina and have a similar effect to alcohol. Their use in sport is subject to certain restrictions. They are completely banned in some sports.
- **Effects** Users maintain a slow heart rate and low blood pressure, used as a relaxant, useful in tense situations. They also have the effect of steadying the hand, important to competitors in target sports. The calming effect can also help in high-risk sports where speed is involved.
- **Side effects** Reduces the heart rate so much that there is a danger that the heart may stop.

Beta blockers are banned in snooker. Here, Peter Ebdon bridges to make a shot.

●●●● ▶ **Active Challenge**

With a partner, study the information on banned substances for several minutes. Now test each other on the categories, names and effects they have on a sportsperson.

Masking agents

These are drugs taken to hide the presence of another drug. Some **masking agents** do not appear on the list of banned substances for particular sports, so their presence is legal. The masking agent hides the presence of a banned substance, which would otherwise disqualify the performer. Substances used for this effect are epitestosterone, probenecid and diuretics, which mask the presence of anabolic steroids.

4 Banned Method

Blood doping is a banned method of improving performance that does not involve the use of drugs. For endurance athletes, the ability of the blood to carry oxygen is crucial to their performance and blood doping aims to improve this. The more oxygen delivered to the working areas of the body the better the results.

Blood can be used from the competitor or from another donor. Two to three months before the competition, blood is removed from the competitor. This gives time for the natural blood reserves to be replenished. The plasma and red blood cells are separated. The plasma is immediately re-injected and the red blood cells are put in cold storage. This blood is then injected back into the body, one week prior to the event. The extra blood in the body has the effect of increasing the amount of red blood cells present and therefore improving the oxygen-carrying capacity, benefiting the athlete's aerobic endurance. An athlete can improve performance by 20% from accurately using this method.

With blood doping there is a threat of blood clots and the blood pressure in the body increases and overloads the circulatory system, putting an unusual and dangerous strain on the heart. There is also the problem, when injecting, of transmitting infectious diseases such as hepatitis and Aids.

What to do:

1. From the information on drugs, create a matrix using the following headings:
   Type of drug
   Drugs in this category
   Which athletes may use it?
   Effect on the athlete
   Side effects/dangers

5 Drugs Testing

All top-class sportspeople are tested for drugs. For example, after each of the 2002 World Cup matches in Korea and Japan, random drugs tests were carried out on players from each of the teams. In national athletics, drugs testing is carried out at several different times:

- in a national event
- in an international event
- at random
- on achieving a world record time or distance, even in training
- on those achieving the first three places in an event
- in training (this is to guard against the athlete who takes performance-enhancing drugs in training but weans themselves off them by the competition date).

Drug testing procedure

- An athlete is chosen for the test.
- The athlete chooses a chaperone, of the same sex, for the test who stays with them at all times. The athlete also chooses a witness, usually their coach or manager.
- The athlete gives a urine sample, witnessed by their coach or manager, and then pours samples into small bottles labelled A and B.
- These samples are then correctly labelled, packed up and locked with a special seal.
- The drugs testing officials completely oversee the whole procedure.
- The samples are then sent to the laboratory for testing. Sample A is tested. Any competitor who refuses to be tested is treated as though they gave a positive sample.

Procedure for positive results

- Governing body of the sport and the competitor informed.
- Governing body investigates the matter. At this stage, the competitor is asked for their account and sample B may be tested.
- An official hearing is arranged by the governing body at which a legal team may defend the competitor.
- If guilty, a penalty is imposed, which varies depending on the type of drug and the sport. Generally a first offence leads to a two-year ban and a second offence has a life ban imposed.
- Any medals or awards achieved at the time of the sample, or after, are taken away from the competitor.

The problem for athletes is that certain banned substances are found in common foods and medicines. Tea and coffee contain caffeine; flu, headache and asthma tablets all contain some banned substances. It is important that the coach checks anything taken by the performer as any illegal substance in the athlete's body, however innocently taken, is treated as a performance enhancer.

Accused athletes have the right to defend themselves against allegations. Diane Modahl, a British athletics champion, was banned for four years, in 1992, after it was claimed she tested positive for a banned performance-enhancing substance. The suspension was lifted after she won a lengthy legal fight to clear her name.

Procedure for negative results

If no drugs are found then no action is taken and the sample B is destroyed. The governing body of the sport and the competitor are informed.

What to do:

1. State the three reasons why the IOC bans performance-enhancing drugs.

2. Make a brief list of 12 stages of a drugs test. Include in the list what happens in the case of both a positive and negative test.

Key Terms:

Blood doping	► method of increasing the oxygen carrying capacity of the blood
Drugs	► substances (other than food) which have a physiological effect when taken into the body
Masking agent	► a legal substance for a sport, hiding the presence of an illegal one
Performance-enhancing drugs	► substances that artificially enhance personal characteristics and performance

Summary

Taking drugs has an effect on the body and mind of a person. Some of these effects are useless to the sportsperson. However, through research, some drugs are seen to have a beneficial effect on performance. Some sportspeople are tempted to break the rules of the governing bodies as they see only the rewards of their drug abuse. By taking some drugs the health of the performer can be seriously endangered. Regulations and procedures are put in place by the governing bodies of each sport to help and guide the performer to make an ethical choice. The sporting authorities want athletes to be safe, sport to have a good name and competition to remain fair.

6 Hygiene

Keeping clothing clean can prevent it from spreading bacteria. This can prevent skin complaints and rashes. After exercising it is always important to shower. Changing into a completely clean set of clothes is refreshing and healthy too. Wearing clean socks and washing feet regularly prevent foot infections starting.

Athlete's foot is a fungus affecting the skin. It develops when someone wears dirty socks or sweaty training shoes. It makes the feet smell and the skin flake between the toes. This causes uncomfortable irritation and itching. Washing feet regularly, drying between toes and wearing clean socks can prevent this infection. Using foot powder from the chemist can prevent and treat athlete's foot.

Verrucas are viral warts, usually on the feet, transmitted in moist areas. Swimming pools are common places to be infected. Verrucas are painful and walking on the infected area can hurt. Wearing a verruca sock can prevent infection or prevent infection spreading; they can be treated by creams, or they can be removed medically.

Prevention of Injury

What you will learn about in this section

1. How to Prepare for Safety in Sport
2. Assess the Risks for Self and Others
3. Coaching and Training
4. Dressing Safely
5. Attitude and Etiquette
6. How the Rules and Officials Help
7. Reducing the Risk in Specific Activities
8. Three Parts to an Exercise Session

All players have a responsibility to prepare well for their chosen event. By listening to their coach and completing their training programme, they learn the rules and **techniques** of the activity. From experience, they build up an understanding of the risks and hazards of the chosen sport and can learn to avoid them in the competition. The rules help to keep the play safe and prevent unfair play.

1 How to Prepare for Safety in Sport

In contact sports there are rules that keep similar age groups together and that separate the sexes at certain ages. This is an attempt to make the competition even and safe by keeping the experience and strength of the players at a similar level. Different factors are taken into account to ensure a **balanced competition**, these include:

- grading
- skill level
- weight
- age
- sex.

2 Assess the Risks for Self and Others

With any game, competitive activity or adventurous pursuit, there are potential dangers. Participants should be prepared properly for the event and trained for skill, strength and tactics. Coaching, training and experience build up knowledge and an awareness of the sport makes the game safer to play. Some dangers are easier to spot than others. In body contact sports, the risk of injury is plain to see. In racket sports there are dangers too. In squash, for example, the confined area could lead to collisions with the opposition and a squash ball just fits in the eye socket!

An even match ensures a good competition. France's Christine Cicot and Great Britain's Karina Bryant during the 2000 Olympics.

Warming-up before an event is vital to train the mind and prepare the body and so reduce the risks. Warm-ups in the winter may have to be extended and extra clothes worn to get the body in the correct condition for competition because of the colder temperatures.

Changes in the environment may cause extra risks. Working in the winter will change the way a training session is conducted. The daylight is gone more quickly, so the timing of training may change or be moved indoors. New safety considerations must also be taken into account, as working surfaces may become wet and icy making them slippery to train on. Athletes should be aware of the need to change their footwear to combat the conditions or the session should be moved indoors.

In the winter, the standard and condition of facilities may drop, for example, maintenance of **throwing cages** may not be scheduled out of season. Landing areas may not be kept and dug over properly. For athletes training for throwing events, especially shot and discus, wet weather makes the equipment slippery and hard to control.

In hotter weather, **dehydration** is an issue. The good weather may encourage people to train more frequently and overuse injury may occur.

 **Active Challenge**

With a partner, choose a sport. Think of as many risks as possible related to that sport. Use examples from television, personal experience and incidents told to you.

3 Coaching and Training

Coaching is essential to all levels of sport. The coach is responsible for giving the performer an understanding of the game. The skills learned will be within the laws of the game and prepare the player for competition. The correct techniques are learned, not only for success but for risk prevention: this is especially important for tackles and lifts.

Training improves the body so it is strong enough to deal with the stresses of the event. This reduces the possibility of fatigue, which often leads to injury. Coaching trains the performer to complete skills in a technically correct way. Body alignment is important in take-offs and landings, especially in activities like gymnastics, trampolining and volleyball, to reduce the risk to the bones and tissues of the body. Knowledge and experience of how to control the equipment for the activity comes about through training. A hockey stick used without training can become a danger to all on the pitch, not just the opposition.

Good lifting technique   **Poor lifting technique**

Using the correct techniques can reduce the risk of injury.

The clothing for team events not only gives a feeling of unity to the group but it can also play its part in safety. Each sport has a unique type of clothing, which has developed due to the nature of the game. It may allow protective guards underneath or be close fitting so it does not catch on equipment. Importantly, it provides free movement so the full range of skills can be performed in each sport. Clothing should:

- be in good order
- not catch on equipment
- ensure the performer can keep a clear view ahead
- not flap in the opposition's face and hinder their performance
- allow free movement to perform the skills of the game.

Sports equipment and clothing should be checked regularly. Repairs should be made so that there is nothing to act as a hindrance or danger to anyone. The correct design of equipment should be used for the job. Specialised equipment should always be worn properly. Loose straps and poorly fitting helmets can be a danger.

Footwear to fit the event

Footwear is a specialised part of sports gear, each sport has its own design. Some sports have several different technical designs to suit a variety of conditions. The correct footwear helps in many ways: it gives support, protection, grip, greatest or least amount of movement and is an aid to performance and streamlining.

The condition of studded footwear should be smooth so that studs do not cut into another player. Checking studs is the job of a referee at the beginning of the game and linesmen can be seen checking the studs for football substitutes. There are specific rules set out in certain sports in which some footwear may be seen as dangerous. It is therefore essential to keep footwear in good order.

What to do:

1. Study the pictures above. Notice that each sport has a different kind of footwear.
2. Say which sport is shown in each picture.
3. Give a reason why the footwear has been developed in that way for each sport.

> Look at the differences in the sole, strapping, material and weather conditions.

Task 1

Protect and be safe

Each activity needs its own protective equipment. Each item of protection guards against a different kind of injury. These injuries could take the form of: impact of another player, the playing surface, the ball, external conditions, forces put on the body by lifting, friction caused by repeating the skills of the event.

What to do:

1. Choose a type of sportsperson and list the items they would need to dress for safety.

Use the pictures above to help with this task.

▶ **Active Challenge**

With a partner, discuss and decide on as many items of protection in as many sports as possible. Now link each item of protection with an incident that could happen in a game.

Work down from head to toe, thinking of the protection a player may need.

Jewellery

Before a team game begins, players are checked for any jewellery they may be wearing. This may seem petty, but each type of jewellery has its own hazards. Sometimes players put a plaster over ear-rings so they are not as dangerous. In games where physical contact regularly occurs, it is essential that there is no jewellery to mark the wearer or the opposition.

- Rings – if fingers are jarred or a ball knocks the end of the finger (called 'stumped finger') the finger swells, a ring could be stuck on the finger and cut into the flesh. Also rings could get caught and cut the performer or an opponent.
- Necklaces – if caught and pulled could cause a scar around the neck.
- Earrings – if caught could injure the wearer or an opponent.

Personal presentation

Finger nails need to be clipped to prevent catching and scarring, especially in games like netball and basketball in which reaching for the ball around head height is common.

Hair should be tidy and not in the performer's eyes so players can see where they are going and it does not flick into another player's eyes.

If glasses are worn they should be made of plastic so if they break they do not shatter and injure someone.

Clothing worn for sport should be kept in good order. Ripped or frayed clothing can catch and be a danger.

Having tidy hair and short finger nails reduces the risk of injury. Here, the USA national football team display their impeccable personal presentation.

5 Attitude and Etiquette

Etiquette is the unwritten code of behaviour a player stands by when competing. Each sport has its own code of behaviour. A general example of this is shaking hands before and after a game. In tennis, new balls are used after the first seven games and every nine games after that; it is not a rule, but it is good etiquette for the player about to serve to show the ball to the opposition by raising it in the air.

A player may throw or kick the ball away in anger after a decision by the referee. This demonstration of bad sportsmanship can be punished by the referee in an attempt to discourage such behaviour from other players.

Taking part is more important than winning!

Play to win!

Judo players bow before a contest.

Tennis players shake hands after a match.

What to do:

1. Read the two columns of part sentences below.
2. Link the beginnings of sentences with the endings.
3. When the sentences are complete, write them in your book.

Beginning of a sentence

1. Players are checked for
2. If a ball jars a finger,
3. Long fingernails can catch and scar,
4. Keeping a sports kit washed
5. Having sweaty and dirty feet
6. Keeping feet clean and dry between the toes
7. Verrucaes are viral warts,
8. Verrucaes can be treated quickly by being removed,
9. Etiquette is an unwritten code of behaviour
10. Shaking hands at the beginning and end of a match

Ending of a sentence

a. which spread in moist areas like swimming baths.
b. so the rules of netball state they should be short.
c. a player, wearing a ring, could cut their flesh.
d. is good etiquette.
e. can stop athlete's foot.
f. jewellery before a game.
g. players keep to for the good of the sport.
h. stops the spread of bacteria.
i. or over time with cream.
j. causes athlete's foot.

Key Terms:

Balanced competition	▶ grouping based on size, age or experience for an even match
Dehydration	▶ extreme lack of water in the body
Etiquette	▶ unwritten and unofficial codes of practice followed in an activity
Technique	▶ way in which a skill is performed

Each game has its own set of rules or laws. These rules are connected to the type of equipment and competition involved. They are designed to make the event safer and fairer. Its set of rules helps to give the game its own individual style.

The governing bodies of the sports make the rules. The players play to the rules. The referee, umpire or judge makes sure the rules are kept. Within the rules are a series of stages of discipline; often the player is given one warning to stop any bad play. If the foul play continues, a player will be asked to leave the game.

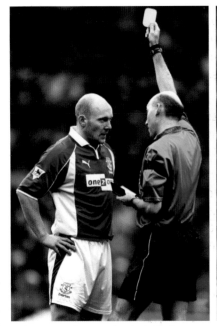

Yellow card; first warning in football for foul play. Thomas Gravesen is shown the yellow card.

Red card; a second yellow (or violent act) earns a red card. Dennis Wise is ordered off.

In rugby and ice hockey, players are sent by the referee to 'cool down' in the sin bin.

In football, red card offences lead to disciplinary hearings where further action may be taken by the Football Association. It is in the player's best interests to obey the rules. Players may lose their competitive edge if the thought of another yellow card, and therefore a sending off, is a possibility.

Officials make sure that there is safe and fair play. When the whistle blows, the game should stop immediately to prevent any further **infringements** and dangerous play. The referee is impartial and makes decisions according to the rules.

Referees make decisions on the spur of the moment and from where they are standing. In professional games, these verdicts are made under the extreme pressure of hundreds of fans who have their own viewpoints on the referee's decisions!

Players have a responsibility to follow the instructions of the officials and to carry on with the game as soon as possible. The flow of the game needs to be maintained and by getting on with the game quickly a surprise attack can begin. This can be especially successful if the other team is still concentrating on the incident.

Rules support referees in their jobs. In rugby, for instance, the 10-yard rule stops players arguing and using foul language.

Umpires use hand signals so that everyone can see clearly the decision made.

What to do:

1. Write down four different responsibilities of a referee.

2. Choose four games or activities. For each one write down a rule that attempts to prevent injury.

> Think of how the referee deals with rules, players and safety.

7 Reducing the Risk in Specific Activities

Venues

There are certain safety requirements a club must fulfil. These are to do with the safety of the sports area and safety for the spectators. People watching the event should be managed properly and be able to watch the match without intimidation from other supporters. The St John Ambulance Brigade attend large venues to deal with any first aid requirements necessary.

There are strict guidelines to do with venue exits, making sure the spectators are able to leave the venue safely. The players should also be able to play their game without fear of the crowd invading the pitch. In top-class events, stewards and police play a part in ensuring the players' safety.

The club is also responsible for the state of the playing surface. The ground should be level, have no litter or sharp objects on the ground, have correct netting and corner flags, safe surface – not slippery, free from protruding objects and so on. The playing surface condition may change due to the weather, so guidelines are pre-stated so officials are able to make the most appropriate decision.

What to do:

1. Study the picture on the previous page. There are 12 hazards shown.

2. Record the hazards and the injury each one could cause.

> It will help to think about personal presentation.

Specialised equipment

Using the correct equipment for the type of user is important for safety. Having equipment that is too big or too heavy could lead to injury and risk. The equipment should suit the size, age and experience of the user.

Invasion, striking and racket games

The size of the equipment should relate to the age and experience of the performer. Using full-size footballs for under elevens, for example, will not match the strength and skill of the players.

There are many **modified games**, which resemble the full game but have been adopted for a younger age group. These games have lighter equipment, smaller playing areas, smaller team numbers and simple rules.

Adapting the rules of the full game makes participation possible for all ages.

Gymnastics

Whether training or competing, the landing areas should be safe and stable. Competition landing areas are 120–200mm thick and have safety mats around them to a depth of 22mm–60mm. The landing, after a vault, for instance, needs to be technically correct for a good overall mark and also for the safety of the performer. A two-footed landing on the toes, cushioning the force of landing, reduces the risk of a jarring injury to the back. The safety requirements for landing areas are set out by the governing body.

The supports for the **asymmetric bars** and their fixings into the floor are specialised and fitted by professionals. This ensures they can withstand the forces put on them by gymnasts during practice and competition.

Equipment in school should be checked by a teacher before work starts. The correct technique should be taught for lifting and lowering vaulting boxes so back injuries are avoided.

A hall set out for a gymnastic training session.

Each piece of equipment must be set out so that it does not interfere with any other piece.

When using a trampoline, the setting out and putting away of this equipment should follow strict guidelines and always be supervised. The weight, size and tension of the trampoline are potentially dangerous.

Dance

The surface the dance is performed on should always be safe and non-slippery. It should be smooth with no splinters. Costumes reflecting the dance and adding drama to the performance should be fitted to each performer securely and allow free movement during the event.

Athletics

All surfaces to run on, throw from and jump off should be flat and free from obstacles and protruding objects.

Throwing events, such as the discus and hammer, require netting or a cage around the throwing area. These should be maintained regularly to prevent equipment escaping through gaps in the fencing. The throwing area should be clearly marked and marshalled. As the competition begins, warnings should be sounded to alert other judges, marshals and competitors that the throw is about to commence.

In jumping events, guidelines for the size, depth and composition of the landing areas are regulated by the governing body. Mats should have a continuous covering over them to keep them together. Throughout the high jump and pole vault competition a check should be kept on the correct placement of the landing area in relation to the bar.

Some equipment is dangerous, the javelin being an obvious example. There are special carry cages and trolleys for transporting awkward equipment. In schools, the training and drilling of moving such equipment, especially javelins and shot, should be reinforced in every lesson.

The throwing cage protects people at the event from a miss throw. Dean Macey prepares to throw.

Equipment, such as javelins, needs to be stored correctly for safety reasons. Steve Backley selects a javelin.

Swimming

All safety information and equipment should be clearly on display at the pool side. Any change of depth in the pool should be clearly marked on the pool edge and visible on the wall too.

The surface around the pool should be non-slip and clean to prevent injury and infection.

Although it may be seen as unglamorous, the swimming cap is a safety aid in a variety of ways. It keeps hair out of the eyes, giving a clear view of the direction for the swimmer and it keeps hair out of the swimmer's mouth, allowing clear, unhindered breathing. Keeping the hair in a cap also helps prevent loose hair entering and blocking the filters.

Although a verruca can be painful, a person can still swim: they must take care when changing so they do not infect the floor and should wear a verruca sock when swimming to prevent it spreading.

Wearing goggles allows the swimmer to see underwater when their face is submerged. This allows turns to be made safely. Goggles also protect the eyes from the chemicals in the water.

NO running.
NO fighting.
NO bomb-diving.
NO young children unsupervised.

Outdoor and adventurous activities

Personal equipment

The clothing taken on any adventurous activity should suit every kind of weather possibility. The clothing mountaineers take on an expedition should be appropriate for any extreme conditions that they might face. These clothes range from under-garments to the outer layers. Boots should be comfortable and sturdy, with a good grip. An activity may begin in warm and sunny weather but, as the day goes on, the weather may change. As the altitude rises the temperature drops on hills and mountains. Experienced mountaineers will be well equipped for this.

In addition to a compass and map a mountaineer may carry the following:

Personal safety kit:

- extra warm clothing
- extra gloves
- food and water
- bivvy bag (waterproof bag large enough for two people to shelter from the elements)
- whistle – for distress call (a mobile phone would help but there are some areas where a signal cannot be picked up)
- torch.

Personal first aid kit:

- 2 crepe bandages: 1 ankle, 1 knee-size tubular bandage for sprains
- army knife with scissors
- sterile wipes for dirty wounds
- various-sized plasters
- 12 pack of swabs for compression
- 1 roll of tape for holding the swabs in place
- safety pin.

Safety equipment

The ability to use a map and compass properly needs specialist training and much practice. If walking over a long distance and in hostile terrain then it is important to be able to navigate. A route plan should be worked out before the party sets off. The plan should include escape points at certain parts of the route so if there is an accident or the weather deteriorates then they can be used. When visibility is zero, owing to the mist coming down, it is possible, as long as you know your position, to navigate with map and compass alone.

The safety equipment should suit all possible conditions of the day. This equipment may be bulky to carry, but it can be shared between members of the group. Often it will not be used but it is there should it be needed. If walking in the winter, specialised equipment is essential for safety, like crampons and ice-axes. Training and experience are necessary so that they can be used properly.

Regular checks on the condition of the equipment should be made. Ropes do not last for ever; they have a life determined by the number of hours used. After this time they cannot be relied on to do their job and so should not be used for climbing again.

Wearing the correct gear and carrying appropriate safety apparatus protects the performer from extreme elements and hazardous situations.

External forces

Before setting out on any expedition a detailed weather report should be studied. The Met Office can supply this for the British Isles. The weather at sea or in the mountains can change rapidly, so preparations should be made accordingly. By obtaining the weather report, predictions can be made as to whether it is viable to go out in the first place or what possible weather changes may occur during the day. If the elements are too much to handle, then it is sensible to turn back or take a safety route home. In mountainous areas the weather can bring wind, mist, rain, snow, heat, sun and storms all in the same day. The key is to prepare for the worst.

Experience of the leader and the crew

A major factor in the safety of the party is the experience, knowledge and ability of the leaders. They should plan the route taking into account the ability of each member of the group. They should have expertise in the use of a map and compass, carry safety equipment and know the safety procedures.

Leaders should be able to assess the group, encourage the weaker members and be able to adapt the pace to suit the whole party. Their ability to make correct decisions under pressure to suit a situation can help ensure the safety of the party. For long expeditions leaders should have the personal ability to keep the morale of the group high, even in difficult and demanding conditions.

Environmental conditions

- Does the sailor/canoeist know the tides and currents?
- Wind may blow the party off course. Rain may dampen morale. Is the group equipped for snow?
- In mist, would they still know where they were going?
- In a storm, would they know what to do?
- Are they prepared for the heat?

Planning the activity

- Is the plan accurate?
- Are there any escape routes?
- Does the route include rests?
- Is it suitable for all members of the group?
- Will it stretch the abilities of the group too far?

Experience of the leaders

- Do they know the area?
- Have they planned the route?
- Are they experienced in safety procedures?
- Can they use the safety equipment they have?
- Can they motivate the group?
- Will they set the speed to the pace of the slowest member?

FACTORS AFFECTING THE SAFETY OF AN OUTDOOR ACTIVITY

Condition of the equipment

- Is that rope too old?
- Is there a record of the equipment's use?
- Is that compass still reliable?
- Is someone taking the correct map?
- Has that torch got good batteries?
- Is the equipment in good order?

Experience of the party

- Are they fit enough? Have they got the correct equipment?
- Have they enough experience for the degree of difficulty they may face?
- Have they the skills to finish the expedition?
- Do they know what is expected of them?

Degree of difficulty of the activity

- Is the group able to complete the route?
- Has the group got the correct equipment for the route?
- Will safety be compromised due to the difficulty?
- Is the route too difficult for the conditions?
- Are group members strong enough to canoe the distance?
- Has everyone got enough and the right kind of protection for the climb?

Task 6

What to do:

1. Compile a list of outdoor and adventurous activities.
2. Name two specialised pieces of equipment required for each activity.
3. Write two sentences about the job of the safety equipment.

> Use the photographs in this section to help you.

> Use reference books or the Internet to help you.

An exercise session consists of a **warm-up**, a **main activity** and a **cool down**.

Warm-up

There are three phases to a warm-up: aerobic phase; stretch and flexibility phase; skills and intensive exercise phase.

The time immediately before the main activity is crucial. This is the period when the body can prepare for rigorous physical activity. There is no set time for a warm-up. It should be adapted to the demands of the sport and the age of the performer.

By warming-up, the body systems, muscles and joints gradually become used to working harder. This gradual increase of stress on the body reduces the risk of injury. The pulse and body temperature are raised to nearer the working rate.

Concentrating on the warm-up activities will concentrate the mind. By focusing in this way an advantage may be gained over the opposition by having a better start to a match.

In the warm-up phase of team sports there needs to be an opportunity to practise the basic skills of the game and start to think collectively as a team. The warm-up creates a link between rest and the main activity. The timing between the two is important. If there is too long a gap the effects of the warm-up will be lost. If actions stressing the muscles and joints, like sprinting, are used in the event then these should be included at the end of the warm-up session.

Types of movement to include in a warm-up

Light aerobic work

This type of activity, such as marching on the spot, starts a session in order to get the heart and lungs working harder.

Stretches

Stretches and flexibility exercises are next. Stretches ease the muscles and joints used in the activity into action.

There are different types of stretches and those performed in the warm-up should, for safety, be performed in the following order:

● static ● assisted ● dynamic.

Athletes using static stretches ease the muscle gradually into the stretched position and hold it there for 10 seconds.

Assisted stretching is when the action is helped by pushing against another person or a wall. A specialised way of stretching is often used in gymnastics. Here, the coach helps the performer by pushing the limb and so stretching the joint further. These are called 'proprioceptive neuromuscular facilitation (PNF) techniques'. These should only be undertaken by an expert and with great care.

After the aerobic phase, static stretches should follow in a warm-up.

Dynamic stretches are the most complex to perform. Care needs to be taken as injury can occur if these are misused. The athlete moves into the stretch position and 'bounces' the muscle. This starts at half pace for two to three repetitions. These gradually increase to full speed. These movements are used when the event or activity needs rapid, explosive movement.

Flexibility exercises

These exercises increase the mobility of the joints of the body – rotating shoulders and hips, for example. Each joint should be given some time, although certain sports may need some joints warmed more than others.

Skills and intensive exercises

Basic skills related to the sport can help co-ordination in a game. The exercises gradually increase in intensity. If the sport includes times when bursts of pace are necessary then, at the end of the session, some short sprints can be included. By warming-up, a person will increase their awareness and reaction time ready for the game. Preparing the body will increase the level of work the person is capable of producing in the event. Note that professional football teams have set warm-ups, which they perform on the pitch before a match.

Main activity

The warm-up leads to the main activity. This can be a training session, skills session or a competition, match or performance. Once the body systems are trained they become fit enough to complete the skills practised. When the body is pushed to the limit in competition, the skills can be put to the test without breaking down because of inadequate fitness levels.

Cool down

There are two phases to the cool down: gentle aerobic and stretching.

After the main activity, the body is given the chance of gradually returning to its resting state; the cool down helps to do this. The heart and muscles of the body take advantage of this. By completing a cool down the heartbeat reaches its resting rate sooner; this is called the 'recovery time'. The heart, therefore, does not have to work too hard for longer than it needs to. The speed of the recovery rate is influenced by several factors:

● The older a person is, the slower the recovery rate will be.
● If the exercise is new, then the new stresses will be harder to recover from.
● How 'in shape' the performer is: the fitter a person is, the quicker the recovery.
● Women tend to recover more slowly than men.

Like the warm-up, there is no set time for a cool down. By keeping the blood circulating it does not have the chance to 'pool' or collect in areas of the circulatory system; this prevents light-headedness.

Gentle stretching stops the build-up of lactic acid in the muscles and so prevents immediate cramp and aching and soreness the following day. Stretches in a cool down should be held for about 30 seconds and should concentrate on the muscles used in the event. Freestyle swimmers will concentrate on cooling down their arms; runners will stretch their legs. A controlled, restful cool down can have a calming effect on a person after the excitement of a competitive match.

What to do:

1. Give three reasons why a warm-up helps a performer.
2. List three types of exercise that would be included in a warm-up.
3. Draw a spidergram of the main points and reasons for a cool down.

Key Terms:

Asymmetric bars	► a piece of gymnastic equipment used by females with bars at different heights
Cool down	► exercises after the main activity gradually bringing the body systems back to a near resting state
Infringement	► action in a game that breaks the rules
Main activity	► period of training, competition or performance when all-out effort is applied
Modified games	► a game with adapted rules, equipment and playing area based on a full game
Throwing cage	► a secured enclosure around a throwing area
Warm-up	► exercises putting greater stresses on the body systems so they are prepared for the main activity

Summary

With most activities there are risks involved and these increase if the competition is not equally matched. Through training and coaching players are made aware of the risks of the activity. Experience helps performers to predict and avoid hazardous situations.

Each sport or activity has its own physical demands. Training for the event prepares the body and its systems for the requirements of the activity. After training, the performer should have the right levels of strength, skill and stamina to compete more safely in the activity. By being able to use the correct technique when playing shots, landing, tackling and dodging, for instance, the player is less likely to suffer injury.

The rules are designed to allow the game to continue in a fair and safe way. Umpires, referees and judges make sure the rules are kept during the competition. They also ensure the conditions are safe, the equipment is set up correctly and whether the venue is suitable for the event when conditions change.

For most activities there is specially designed equipment. Some is designed to carry out the game and some for the safety of the performers. Both types should be kept in good condition as their effectiveness may be reduced if they are damaged in any way. For instance, if helmets are cracked they lose their protective quality. Whatever safety equipment is used, it should be worn correctly and strapped on properly.

Italian volleyball player Luca Cantagalli wears knee pads for protection.

Sports Injuries

What you will learn about in this section

1. Minor Injuries
2. Common Injuries
3. Major Injuries
4. Head and Awareness Problems
5. Dangers from the Environment

There are minor and major risks of injury involved with most sports. There is less risk of injury in sports where teams stay on their side of a net, like volleyball and badminton. The risks increase in contact sports where players invade the territory of the other team. The rules and nature of the sport may present safety problems. The weather may play a part in increasing the risk or technical problems may occur.

The following pages contain the procedures for dealing with a series of injuries. Only trained and qualified first aid and medical personnel should deal with serious injuries.

Expert training cannot always prevent injury.

The nature of the game can cause injuries.

1 Minor Injuries

All people who take part in sport will occasionally suffer from minor injuries. They are easy to deal with and treat, usually using a combination of ice, antiseptic wipes, plasters and dressing is enough. It is important to treat injuries quickly to prevent them from becoming worse and more of a major problem.

The minor injuries ready reckoner

Bruises	Cuts	Abrasions/Grazes	Blisters
soft tissue skin damage	soft tissue skin damage	soft tissue skin damage	soft tissue skin damage
How it happens			
impact with equipment, floor or player	studs, collision with sharp object	skin rubs against rough surface	continual rubbing of skin against another surface
When it might happen			
during a tackle, landing and interception	during a tackle	fall, sliding tackle, friction with other objects on ground, against wall (squash), AstroTurf	badly fitting boots, running on hard surfaces
Where it could happen			
muscles of the body	on the surface of the skin	on the surface of the skin	on heels from shoes rubbing, on hands from rowing, using asymmetric bars, or bow drawn in archery
Effect on the body			
blood vessels damaged beneath the surface = bruise, colour goes blue/purple to green/yellow	bleeding	pain at injury, grit can often enter the wound, top layer of skin removed	thin bubbles of salty liquid form under the skin
What to do			
put ice on the injured area reducing swelling	clean and dress with plaster, add bandage if a bad cut, if worse go to hospital	clean wound and dress	keep the blister intact, as this is a natural, sterile covering; below the blister there is another layer of skin forming to replace the upper one; if blister is likely to be damaged a dressing should be applied that more than covers the area
How to avoid			
avoid collisions and wear protective clothing	wear protective clothing, check equipment, check players for jewellery and the length of their fingernails	wear protective clothing	wear correctly fitting footwear; wear in new boots, spikes or trainers gradually; wear thick, correctly-sized socks; check feet and dress to prevent skin damage

What to do:

1. Write a paragraph about each of the following injuries:

   a. bruise

   b. cut

   c. blister

   d. graze.

> Use the headings from the table on page 87 to help you make sentences.

2 Common Injuries

These injuries are more complex than minor injuries. Although some can be dealt with using basic first aid, some injuries may need expert treatment. Strains and pulls affect the soft tissues of the body; tennis or golf elbow affects the joints.

Use the RICE procedure to treat soft tissue injuries. Each initial stands for part of the treatment.

Rest the injured part.

Rest – prevents further injury.

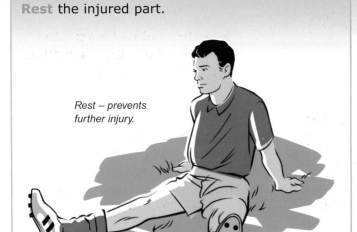

Ice – apply ice to the injured part to stop the swelling and help the pain.

Ice – applied for 10-minute periods stops swelling, pain and flow of blood to area.

Compression – put a bandage around the injured area for support and to stop swelling.

Compression – the bandage is just tight enough to reduce internal bleeding and swelling.

Elevate – lift the injured part to restrict the blood flow to the area and reduce swelling and painful throbbing.

Elevation – raising injured area above level of the heart lowers internal bleeding and stops swelling and throbbing. In some instances raising an injured part slightly is enough to reduce any pressure on it.

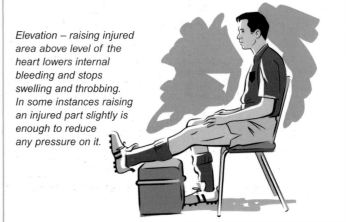

Strain (pulled muscle) – soft tissue injury

How it happens – overstretching of the muscles

When it happens – twist or wrench of the muscle

Where it happens – muscles of the body

Effects on the body – may be weakened as a result

What to do – use RICE

How to avoid – warm-up thoroughly; but, it is difficult to avoid when an activity requires the performer to contract and relax a muscle quickly

Sprain – soft tissue injury

How it happens – ankle or wrist joint twisted suddenly

When it happens – changing direction or landing badly

Where it happens – at the ankle or wrist joint

Effects on the body – tears ligaments at a joint and is extremely painful

What to do – use RICE; if more severe can look like a fracture or dislocation so treat as such and have an x-ray

How to avoid – improve the strength of the area; sometimes it is difficult to avoid

Tennis elbow – overuse injury

How it happens – too much use of the tendons

When it happens – playing tennis or golf; playing with a racket with the wrong-sized handle

Where it happens – at the elbow joint

Effects on the body – inflamed elbow joint

What to do – use RICE or seek medical advice

How to avoid – choose the correct-sized equipment; moderate the amount of play

What to do:

Write out the following paragraphs, filling in the gaps as you go.

1. Strains and sprains are examples of _____ _____ _____. Strains are to do with _____ and sprains are to do with _____ and _____. Each occurs when rigorous over_____ and twisting take place. _____ too far to reach a ball in tennis or _____ at speed in basketball can cause these problems.

2. Both injuries are treated using the RICE procedure. The initials stand for _____, ice, _____ and elevation. The reason to rest the injured part is so that no further_____ is done. By putting ice on the injury it _____ the _____. _____ the part also stops the swelling as does elevating the injured part which stops the _____ too.

3. Tennis and golf elbow affect the _____ attaching the muscle to the bone at the elbow. This can be caused by playing the sport _____ _____ and by using the _____ equipment. Again, RICE is the treatment for this injury.

Task 2

These injuries require expert treatment. Some need surgery, others need special **convalescence**. Such injuries happen when stresses on the body are too much for it to handle. This might be because of changing direction at speed, the impact of another player or collision with equipment. Shock can often result as a reaction, of the casualty or a by-stander, after witnessing a major injury.

Applying pressure to the cut reduces the loss of blood.

Deep cuts

If there is a large or deep cut to the skin, hospital treatment may be necessary. Pressure should be placed on the cut in an attempt to stop the loss of blood. The area of the cut should be elevated. If the blood is pulsating, like the beat of the heart, it indicates that an artery has been damaged. This is a serious condition and an ambulance should be called immediately.

Torn cartilage - soft tissue injury

A torn cartilage happens when a joint is twisted excessively. A player is prone to doing this when changing direction or pivoting at speed. A common area for this injury is at the knee joint. When it happens it is extremely painful when the joint is moved. Treatment for this is RICE. An operation may be necessary in severe cases. Due to the nature of the game this injury is common for footballers. It is hard to avoid an injury of this kind, especially in competitive matches.

Dislocation - hard tissue injury

A **dislocation** occurs when the joint is moved outside its designed range. A forceful blow can move the joint out of position. All major joints are vulnerable. When it happens the joint looks deformed, it will be very painful and the person will have no control over the movement in that area. In these cases the person should be made comfortable, the joint immobilised and medical help found quickly – do not attempt to put the joint back into place. Strength training exercises for the muscles and tissues around the joints will help prevent this happening.

Fractures - hard tissue injury

Fractures occur when an excessive impact or force is put on the bone. This can happen with a blow or a twist. When a bone is fractured, the limb becomes immobile and there is extreme pain. The area is tender and there may be swelling, leading to bruising. The fractured area immediately looks deformed. Fractures are difficult to avoid, as they are a result of spur-of-the-moment accidents. Keeping to the rules of the game and not tackling recklessly reduce the risk of injury.

Open/compound fracture

The broken end of a bone comes through the skin. This causes complications as there is a risk of infection from germs entering where the skin is damaged.

Closed/simple fracture

The break of the bone is under the skin.

In rugby, because of the upper body impact of tackling and falling on an outstretched hand, a fracture of the clavicle is a common injury. When this happens the casualty may automatically cradle the arm on the injured side under the elbow. They may also lean their head to the injured side too.

The impact of two legs meeting with force in a football tackle can cause a fracture. The tibia and fibula (lower leg bones) are the most common leg bones to fracture. If both are broken, the limb will rotate and have an angle at the point of the fracture. If the tibia (shin bone) is broken then there is a possibility that the fracture will be open.

Medical help should be sent for immediately and the casualty should be made comfortable and kept warm without moving the injured part.

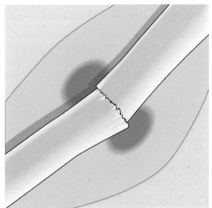

Closed fracture of the tibia.

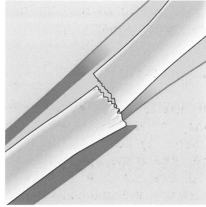

Open fracture of the tibia.

There are several types of fracture, each differing due to the age of the bone and the type of impact, blow or pressure placed on it.

Greenstick

A pressure or impact buckles or bends a bone but only partially breaks it. This fracture is common in the developing bones of young children, whose bones are quite springy.

Transverse

This fracture is the result of a direct blow made at a right angle to a bone, resulting in a break straight across. The name relates to the direction of the break in the bone.

Impacted

In this fracture the two ends of bone are firmly shoved together causing it to fracture. The ends of the bone are misaligned, but pressed together.

Comminuted

Here an impact causes a bone to splinter, resulting in more than two pieces of bone at the site of the injury. This fracture is usually the result of a direct blow on a bone.

Oblique/Spiral

Here the direction of the fracture is diagonal to the length of a bone. It happens when there is a twisting movement along the bone's length, for example if a foot is trapped and the leg twists.

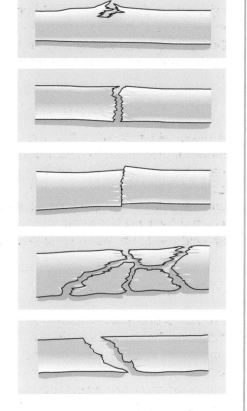

 **Active Challenge**

With a partner, think of sporting occasions where participation might result in each above fractures may happen.

Key Terms:

Compound/Open fracture	▶ break of the bone when the skin is broken
Convalescence	▶ period of time when body is rested to aid recovery
Dislocate	▶ joints moved out of their normal arrangement
Inflamed	▶ reddened and swollen
Simple/Closed fracture	▶ break of the bone when the skin is not broken

Shock - primary

How it happens – in reaction to a traumatic event
When it happens – after witnessing an emotional or traumatic event
Where it happens – at the site of the incident
How to avoid – avoid known causes

Shock - true shock

How it happens – in reaction to injury
When it happens – after serious injury, usually bad cut or fracture
Where it happens – at the site of the accident
How to avoid – difficult to avoid
Effects on the body – pale complexion, quick pulse, cold and clammy skin, **nausea**, thirsty, feeling faint, restlessness, quick gasps for air, aggression, possibly unconscious
What to do – send for medical help, lie person down, lift legs higher than head as this helps the flow of blood to the brain, loosen tight clothing, keep a good air flow around them, keep them warm and calm, keep checking breathing and pulse; if unconscious put in the recovery position

What to do:

1. Create a matrix for the medical conditions torn cartilage, dislocation, fracture and shock.

> Use the minor injuries ready reckoner to help.

Task 3

4 Head and Awareness Problems

There are several causes of unconsciousness. In sport, too much stress on the body systems can cause a heart attack or a stroke, which lead to losing consciousness. There may be an impact on the head or blockage of the windpipe. Any blow to the head is serious. Concussion may result and the effects may only become evident some time after the incident. Medical advice is always necessary.

Recovery position

The purpose of the recovery position is to make the casualty comfortable, safe from falling and further injury, able to breath clearly and safe from choking. It is used on unconscious casualties.

- The chin is lifted to keep airway clear, hand supports head.
- The arm and leg are bent to make position stable.
- The chest is flat on ground, so breathing is easier.

Unconsciousness

How it happens – a blow to the head, heart attack, fainting, stroke, shock, asphyxia
When it happens – impact with another player, raising the pulse too high, blocking or compressing the windpipe
Where it happens – affects the whole body
Effects on the body – a state of unwakening sleep
What to do – send for medical help and place in the recovery position
How to avoid – wear protective equipment and take care in the sport

Emergency procedures

If the casualty has lost consciousness, a sequence of actions should be followed to deal with the situation. Send for medical help. In the time it takes for this help to arrive, put the 'DR ABC' sequence into operation.

Danger

Are you or the casualty in danger?

Response

Is the casualty conscious?

Airway

Is the casualty's airway open? Check there is no blockage of the airway. This may be vomit from the person or another obstacle. Clear the mouth if there is a blockage.

Breathing

Is the casualty breathing? **Look** for the rise and fall of the chest. **Listen** for sounds of breathing. **Feel** for breath on your cheek or condensation on a mirror. If not, apply MMV. If breathing, place in the recovery position.

Circulation
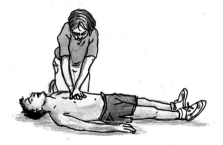
Can you feel the casualty's pulse? If there is a pulse, place in the recovery position. If not, administer CPR.

●●●● ▶ Active Challenge

With a partner, study the illustrations above. Now test each other on the meaning of and procedure for DR ABC.

Mouth-to-mouth ventilation (MMV)

When a person has stopped breathing the following procedure can get vital oxygen into the body artificially and, in some cases, start independent breathing again.

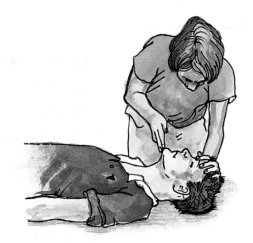

- Turn casualty on their back. If necessary, clear their mouth.
- Keep airway open by lifting the chin and holding the forehead.
- Close the nose by pinching with finger and thumb using the hand on the casualty's forehead.
- Take a deep breath.
- Make a good seal over casualty's mouth so no air can escape.
- Blow out into the mouth for about two seconds. Watch for the chest to rise.
- Remove lips to allow the casualty's lungs to deflate.
- Repeat the procedure once and check circulation.
- Look for breathing, coughing, colour returning.
- If there is circulation, continue and every ten breaths check pulse again.
- Continue until an ambulance arrives, casualty breathes on their own or you are too tired.
- If there is no pulse, administer CPR.

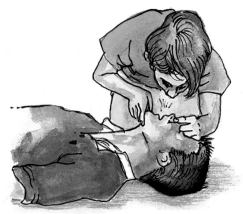

Cardio-pulmonary resuscitation (CPR)

If a person has stopped breathing and has no pulse you will need to administer CPR. The aim of each compression is to squeeze the heart between the sternum and the spine and so pump blood through the body. The following procedure should be followed.

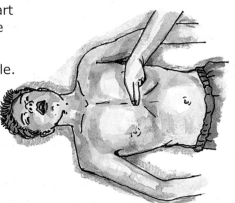

- Place casualty on their back on as hard a flat surface as possible.
- Find bottom ribs with index and middle fingers.
- Keeping fingers together, slide them up to the point where lowest ribs meet the sternum (breast bone).
- Place index finger and middle finger on sternum.
- Slide the heel of your other hand down the breastbone until it meets the index finger.
- Put first hand on top of heel of second hand.
- Interlock fingers, keeping them off the chest.
- Lean over the casualty with arms and elbows in a straight line.
- Position shoulders over the hands so that pressure is exerted straight down.
- Exert pressure on the sternum, ensuring fingers are kept raised.
- Release the pressure, without moving hands from chest, so the heart can refill with blood.
- Keep the movement of the compressions smooth in a down-and -up manner.
- Perform 15 cardiac compressions to every 2 ventilations.
- Continue until the casualty shows signs of life, help arrives or you are too exhausted to carry on.

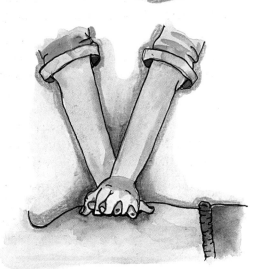

Note both MMV and CPR procedures are different for young children and babies.

Concussion

How it happens – blow to the head

When it happens – games play, physical contact sports, from slipping and falling

Where it happens – head or jaw

Effects on the body – shallow breathing, pale complexion, confusion, dizziness, sickness

What to do – place in the recovery position, stay with victim and seek medical advice; rugby players who have suffered from concussion have a period of time when they cannot compete

How to avoid – care in sport, wear safety and protective equipment

5 Dangers from the Environment

The weather can cause a major problem if a team is not equipped to deal with its changes. Its effects are obvious in adventurous sports, like mountaineering and sailing, but problems can occur even in regular team games situations. The answer is to prepare for possible changes and adapt plans to suit the situation. It is better to prevent the problem happening than have to deal with it.

Hypothermia – extreme environmental injury

How it happens – a rapid drop in the inner core temperature of the body (lungs, heart, brain) below 35°C. The loss of heat from the body is related to the size of the individual and the environment. Generally the bigger a person is, the slower the heat loss. The colder and windier the air the greater the heat loss. Therefore, children will tend to lose heat more quickly and suffer from hypothermia more quickly.

When it happens – inactivity in a cold, wet and windy environment when the energy required is more than the energy available.

Where it happens – any cold environment, hostile mountain areas, sea, river or lake.

Effects on the body – shivering, pale complexion, dry complexion, pulse rate could be slower than normal, shallow breathing, behaviour may be irrational, state of confusion, lack of energy leading to unconsciousness.

What to do – if the casualty is responsive try to make them more mobile, but stopping inactivity will have to be matched by energy intake. If the victim is unresponsive send for help and then take them to a sheltered spot and keep their body from the wet ground. Immediate action is necessary to heat the core of the body: replace wet clothes with warm, dry ones; cover the head; provide a sugary, warm drink; give quick energy food like chocolate. Check pulse and breathing regularly. If available, put the victim into a warm bath, not more than 40°C, to warm the body back up gradually.

How to avoid – when the weather is colder, put on layers of warmer clothes. Be aware of the wind chill factor, which often causes hypothermia. Always take the proper equipment and know the safety procedures. Keep an eye on all members of the party to prevent this happening. Long distance swimmers can use grease to keep the cold out.

Hypothermia starts as shivering.   *The sufferer may become abusive.*   *As more heat is lost, the casualty loses consciousness.*

Dehydration – extreme environmental injury

How it happens – when there is a rapid loss of water from the body

When it happens – training hard, sweating, breathing out water vapour or passing water and not replenishing the water lost

Where it happens – more common in a hot climate or during an endurance event

Effects on the body – tiredness, sickness and dizziness

What to do – replace lost fluid and salt

How to avoid – keep replacing water loss by drinking regularly, particularly when exercising

What to do:

1. Work with a partner and create a crossword using words that indicate a major injury.

   A list of clues are provided to help get you started.

   1. This happens if the knee is twisted excessively. 4, 9
   2. The C in RICE. 11
   3. The bones do this if they are moved out of their normal arrangement. 9
   4. A place where two or more bones meet. 5
   5. The injured part is _____ to stop further damage. 8
   6. Type of fracture. 8
   7. A fractured bone may have _____ around it. 8
   8. Immediate action for a fracture – send for an _____ . 9
   9. Can happen as a reaction to witnessing an injury. 5
   10. The pulse can _____ when suffering from shock. 7
   11. A casualty is placed in this when unconscious. 8, 8
   12. A state of unawakening sleep. 15
   13. The C in DR ABC. 11
   14. Can result from a blow to the head. 10
   15. The V in MMV. 11
   16. Condition resulting from rapid heat loss. 11
   17. What a long distance swimmer uses to stop the cold. 6
   18. Condition resulting from lack of water in the body. 11

Task 4

Wolverhampton Wanderers' goalkeeper Mike Stowell collides with Manchester City's Gareth Taylor.

Summary

There are many injuries that are caused by sport, some in training and some in the game itself. In general, soft tissue injuries, minor cuts and bruises happen frequently and, if treated early, clear up quickly, but if left they can become more serious. Such injuries can usually be treated immediately with basic first aid.

Hard tissue injuries – torn cartilage and broken bones – need specialised medical treatment and a period of rehabilitation so the injury is given time to heal fully and the body to return gradually to fitness.

Shock may occur as a reaction to witnessing or suffering an injury. This condition can show at the time of the injury or hours afterwards. Head injuries should always be treated seriously however minor they seem at the time. Blows to the head may have no immediate effects but could, after time, cause concussion.

Players or performers are sometimes not aware of an injury or condition gradually affecting their bodies, like heat and cold. Knowledge and experience of the event and the effects of the environment are crucial to the well-being of the performer and preventative measures can be taken to counter the dangers.

The Circulatory System

What you will learn about in this section

1 Identifying Parts of the Circulatory System
2 The Heart as the Pump in a Double Circulatory System
3 A Comparison of Different Blood Vessels
4 The Function of Blood at Rest
5 The Effects of Exercise on the Heart
6 The Immediate Effects of Exercise on the Circulatory System
7 The Long-term Effects of Exercise

1 Identifying Parts of the Circulatory System

The **circulatory system** involves the heart, vessels, blood and the **pulmonary** and **systemic circuits**. It is known as the cardiovascular system – cardio meaning heart and vascular relating to blood vessels.

The function of the circulatory system is to:

- Transport oxygen and nutrients to parts of the body and remove waste or toxic products from the body – the body relies on these to keep alive. The balance of nutrients also keeps the body functioning properly.
- Control body temperature – the body is affected by changes of temperature, so keeping it in an acceptable range keeps the body functioning properly.
- Protect – antibodies in the blood fight disease and platelets help to clot the blood at the source of a cut and prevent other germs entering the body.

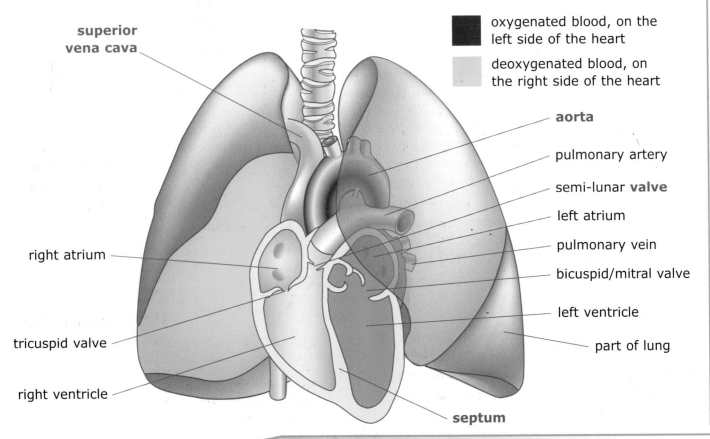

The **pulmonary circuit** carries blood from the heart to the lungs and back again.

The **systemic circuit** carries blood from the heart to the rest of the body and back again.

What to do:

1. Learn the names of the different parts of the circulation system.

> Remember the right side of the heart has the pulmonary vein taking deoxygenated blood away and the left side has the pulmonary artery bringing oxygenated blood back to the heart.

2 The Heart as the Pump in a Double Circulatory System

The heart has four chambers. The right side of the body deals with the blood with less oxygen in it – deoxygenated blood; and the left side has the blood with more oxygen in it – oxygenated blood. The **septum** divides the left and right sides of the heart so that oxygenated and deoxygenated blood do not mix. The left ventricle wall is thicker than the right side. It is more developed as it pumps blood further around the body.

In the heart, sets of **valves** are positioned to stop the back flow of blood. Between the right atrium and ventricle is the tricuspid valve. On the left side between the left atrium and ventricle is the bicuspid valve. The semi-lunar valves are at the exits of both ventricles as they meet the pulmonary artery on the right and the **aorta** on the left.

The pulmonary circuit is a complete circuit that carries blood from the heart to the lungs and back. It moves deoxygenated blood from the right ventricle, via the pulmonary artery and takes it to the lungs. In the lungs it picks up oxygen and thus becomes re-oxygenated. It leaves the lungs by the pulmonary vein to the left atrium of the heart.

The systemic circuit is also a complete circuit. It carries blood from the heart to all parts of the body and back to the heart. The oxygenated blood is pumped from the left atrium to the left ventricle and into the aorta. It travels around the body to be used by the working muscles. The blood, once used, is deoxygenated. It makes its way back to the right atrium of the heart via the **vena cava** to start the cycle over again.

When the heart beats or contracts it is called 'systole'. This action forces blood through the arteries around the body. When the heart relaxes, it fills up with blood returning from the veins. This is called the 'diastole' or 'diastolic phase'.

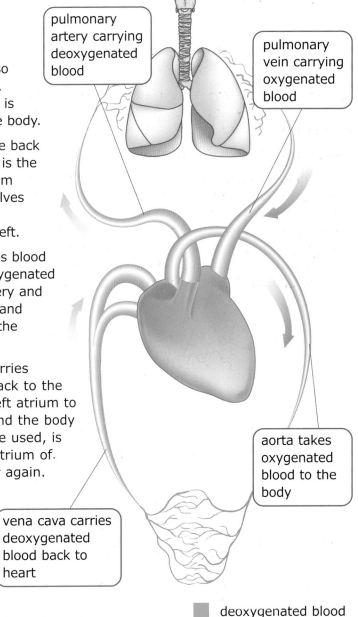

pulmonary artery carrying deoxygenated blood

pulmonary vein carrying oxygenated blood

aorta takes oxygenated blood to the body

vena cava carries deoxygenated blood back to heart

▨ deoxygenated blood
■ oxygenated blood

What to do:

1. Using the diagram above, trace the pathway of blood.
2. Start at the heart, leading into the pulmonary artery.
3. Colour the systemic and pulmonary systems.

> Number parts so they remind you of the order.

Arteries

Arteries carry blood away from the heart. Due to the closeness of some of them to the heart, they have a pulse and work under high pressure. The walls of arteries, therefore, need to be very thick and flexible.

Blood leaves the heart in the aorta, the longest artery in the body. Smaller arteries branch off the aorta, so that the oxygen gets to all parts of the body. In its transportation of blood, it divides into smaller **arterioles** and then into even smaller capillaries. The outer layer of an artery is tough and fibrous. The inner lining (**endothelium**) is elastic. The diameter of the inner layer is controlled involuntarily. It automatically changes size according to the amount of blood flowing at any time.

Capillaries

Arterioles lead in to the capillaries, which are grouped in clusters. Capillaries are the smallest of all the vessels with walls just one cell thick: they are thinner than strands of hair. At one end, they feed muscles, organs and body tissue with oxygen and nutrients. At the other, carbon dioxide and waste products pass through their walls to flow into veins for removal from the body. Blood enters the capillaries under pressure. Capillaries bring blood within reach of every cell. Because substances pass through the walls they are called 'semi-permeable'.

Veins

Capillaries feed the veins. The walls of veins are thinner than arteries. Their function is to bring the dark red, deoxygenated blood back to the heart and they work at lower pressure. They have an inner layer (endothelium) and two tough outer fibrous layers. These are thinner than the arterial layers and less elastic. To help the veins get the blood back to the heart they have valves to stop the blood flowing backwards due in part to gravitational pull. Additionally, pulsating muscles, close to the veins, help to keep the blood moving. This action is called the 'skeletal pump'.

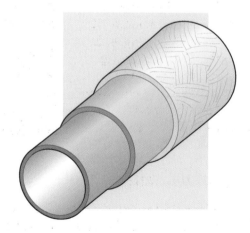

What to do:

1. Make a table of information about the three vessels.

> Look at the above sections on arteries, capillaries and veins. Think about the similarities and differences.

Task 3

Key Terms:

Aorta ► main blood vessel leaving the heart

Arterioles ► blood vessels that are sub-divisions of arteries

Circulatory system ► transports blood using the heart and blood vessels

Endothelium ► internal space of the blood vessels; in arteries this changes according to the amount of blood to be transported

Pulmonary circuit ► transports blood from the heart to the lungs and back again

Septum ► wall of muscle dividing the left and right sides of the heart

Systemic circuit ► transports blood from the heart to the body and back to the heart again

Valves ► openings allowing blood flow in one direction only found in the heart and veins

Vena cava ► blood vessel transporting deoxygenated blood back to the heart

4 The Function of Blood at Rest

Red blood cells

These cells – erythrocytes – are small but there are many of them. Two million are produced and destroyed in your body every second! Their main job is to carry oxygen, but they also transport nutrients and waste products, such as carbon dioxide. They are produced in the bone marrow of long bones.

In these cells is **haemoglobin**. Oxygen chemically attaches itself to it to make oxyhaemoglobin. It is in this way that oxygen is transported to the working muscles of the body and carbon dioxide is taken away to the lungs transported in solution to the plasma.

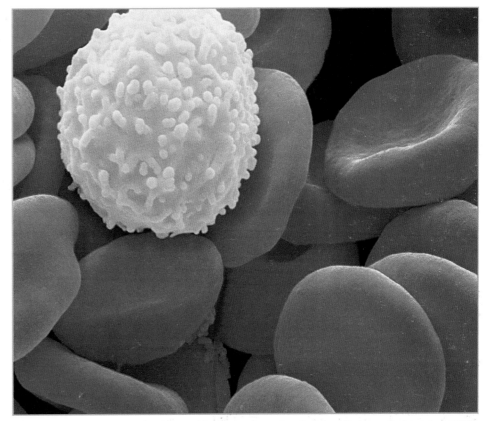

Human blood, showing red and white cells (magnified approx. x3500).

White blood cells

The job of the white blood cells – leukocytes – is to protect the body. There are five types of white blood cells. The main functions of leukocytes are to fight infection at its source, repair damaged tissue and destroy bacteria. When a cut or graze occurs, the white blood cells gather to stop bacteria entering the body. When a scab forms it is made up dead of leukocytes. There are fewer white than red blood cells in the body. The cells are produced in the marrow of bones and lymph tissue of the body.

Platelets

These are small parts of larger cells. They are in charge of clotting the blood. They clot at the skin surface after a graze or cut. They do the same job internally, on small, damaged blood vessels. Clotting is important to stop blood loss from the body and stop internal bleeding.

Plasma

Plasma is made mostly of water. It makes up 55% of the volume of blood. It helps the blood flow easier by the use of plasma proteins. The 10% of plasma that is not water, contains a mixture of the following: salts, chlorine, amino acids, glucose, antibodies, **fibrinogens** (helps clotting), hormones and waste products such as urea and carbon dioxide.

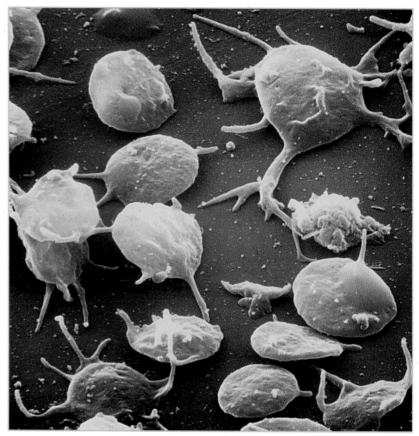

Unactivated blood platelets are oval, whereas activated platelets develop extensions from the cell wall, as seen here (magnified approx. x3300).

What to do:

1. From your knowledge of the composition of blood, copy and complete each sentence.

   a. Red blood cells are called

   b. The main function of red blood cells

   c. Red blood cells contain haemoglobin, this helps

   d. White blood cells protect the body

   e. White blood cells are also called

   f. White blood cells are produced

   g. The job of the platelets is

   h. Platelets are smaller parts

   i. Plasma is 90% water and makes up

   j. Plasma contains plasma proteins that help

Task 4

5   The Effects of Exercise on the Heart

At rest, the heart has a chance to slow down as it does not have to work so hard against gravity to circulate the blood. The **resting heart rate** is about 72 beats per minute, although this varies with gender and age. This is sufficient to supply the muscles with the necessary blood and nutrients. Every heartbeat pumps blood out of the heart; this is called the 'stroke volume'. The total volume of blood pumped out of the heart, calculated over a minute, is called the 'cardiac output'.

The heart rate increases when extra demands are made on the body. The rate depends on the type of activity. If it is easy, the pulse goes up a little; if the activity is more intense, then the pulse rises further.

Performers can regulate the intensity of their training if they know their **maximum heart rate**. Usually, the heart rate needs to be raised to at least 60% of the maximum, to improve cardiovascular fitness levels.

To work out the maximum heart or pulse rate the following formula is used:

220 – age = maximum heart rate

Stroke volume is the amount of blood pumped out of the heart with each beat. At rest, the heart pumps about 85ml of blood. During exercise this could increase to 130ml (nearly a quarter of a pint) depending on fitness levels. This is a lot of blood considering the heart is only the size of a clenched fist.

Cardiac output is the amount of blood ejected from the heart per minute. To work out the cardiac output multiply the stroke volume by the heart rate. As the heart rate and stroke volume increase with exercise so does the cardiac output.

After exercise, the heart returns to its resting rate. The time it takes to do this is referred to as the **recovery rate**. A cool down can help the body gradually return to the resting heart rate. This takes about five minutes depending on the fitness level and type of cool down.

What to do:

1. Create a spidergram showing the effects of exercise on the heart.

6   The Immediate Effects of Exercise on the Circulatory System

Muscles need oxygen to work. This is the key to the circulatory system. In the lungs oxygen combines with haemoglobin in the red blood cells, making oxyhaemoglobin. In this form the red blood cells look bright red. From the lungs the blood transfers oxygen to the working muscles. To supply this demand the heart rate increases. The stroke volume and the cardiac output are both increased during exercise. When exercise starts, the muscles use more energy and so the rates and volume of the heart change. An area in the brain called the 'cardiac centre' controls and regulates how hard the heart works.

Working muscles produce heat

As well as producing movement when they are working muscles also produce heat. Too much heat is bad for the body and can cause **heat exhaustion**. To prevent the body temperature rising blood vessels at the surface of the skin open (**dilate**) and heat is transported away from the body. More waste products are made during exercise. These can interfere with the effective running of the body. Salt and water are such waste products. These exit the body via the pores and capillaries at the surface of the skin.

During exercise, there is a greater need for more blood to circulate around the body. The arteries automatically adapt to this demand. Their internal diameter, called the 'endothelium', automatically widens to let more blood through.

colour changes

blood moved to skin surface for heat regulation

shunting of blood to working muscles

salt loss

heart rate increases

stroke volume increases

cardiac output increases

sweating/ water loss occurs

Active Challenge

Find your carotid pulse at your neck (press your first two fingers to the side of your throat).

Record your resting pulse.

Now jump on the spot for one minute.

Take your pulse again. How has it changed?

Are you showing any other immediate effects of exercise?

Endurance training, commonly known as aerobic training, helps strengthen the heart. This type of training is progressive, over time. With training the general size of the heart gets bigger, the walls become thicker, stronger and more robust. The resting stroke volume increases and so does the cardiac output.

Whilst everything else is increasing, the heart rate does the opposite. A useful indicator of good fitness is the **resting heart rate**. The slower it is per minute, the more efficient the heart is. It can pump the required amount of blood with fewer beats. Therefore, the slower the resting heartbeat, the fitter the person. With good aerobic fitness, a person will usually be able to keep working efficiently without tiring or losing skill.

What to do:

1. Taking regular exercise affects the body in many ways. Using the two headings 'Immediate Effects of Exercise' and 'Long-term Effects of Exercise', make a list of the different changes that happen to the body.

Key terms:

Cardiac output	► the amount of blood pumped by the heart in one minute
Dilate	► open up or become wider
Endurance	► the ability to keep working over a period without tiring or losing skill
Fibrinogen	► a protein found in blood that helps clotting
Haemoglobin	► found in red blood cells, transports oxygen to body tissue
Heat exhaustion	► fatigue brought on by the body temperature rising
Maximum heart rate	► calculated as 220 minus age
Recovery rate	► the time it takes for the heart to return to resting rate after exercise
Resting heart rate	► amount of heart beats per minute when the body is at rest
Stroke volume	► the amount of blood pumped by the heart in one beat

Summary

The contents of blood keep the body alive: the circulation of blood to different parts of the body is vital. Oxygen, nutrients and hormones give the tissues of the body what they need to work. Waste products such as salt, heat, water, carbon dioxide and urea are all removed from the body so it is not poisoned.

When a person exercises, the circulatory system needs to work faster as there is greater demand by the muscles for oxygen. With regular exercise, the body can be trained to make these adjustments quickly and efficiently.

A properly planned personal exercise programme (PEP) should not be too demanding at the start. The PEP will then gradually increase in difficulty or intensity as the person's body adapts to the new stresses. This gradual increase in exercise level will ensure that a person avoids injury and does not place excessive stress on their circulatory system.

The Respiratory System

What you will learn about in this section

1. The Vital Parts of the Respiratory System
2. Role of the Lungs
3. Mechanism of Breathing
4. How Exercise Affects Breathing
5. Aerobic and Anaerobic Activity
6. What Happens to the Body During Exercise and Why?
7. How the Body Recovers from Physical Activity

1 The Vital Parts of the Respiratory System

The function of the respiratory system is to get oxygen into the body and carbon dioxide out of the body. This happens through the act of breathing. Breathing in (inhalation) gets the oxygen in, so it can be used by the body to release energy. Breathing out (exhalation) removes the carbon dioxide so it does not build up and poison the body.

The parts of the respiratory system are:

- air passages
- lungs
- **diaphragm**.

Air passages

The air passages are a series of linking tubes. They create the pathway for the air to get to the lungs. Air can enter the body through the mouth or the nose. Air entering the body through the nose, rather than the mouth, has distinct advantages:

- It is warmed, making it a similar temperature to the internal organs.
- There are hairs and mucus in the nose which filter the air stopping the larger particles of dust and pollen getting into the lungs. The absence of particles allows the **alveoli** to work well.
- The nose moistens the air so it can be absorbed by the alveoli more easily.

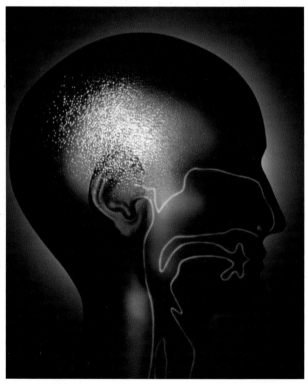

Air passages of the nose and throat outlined in orange.

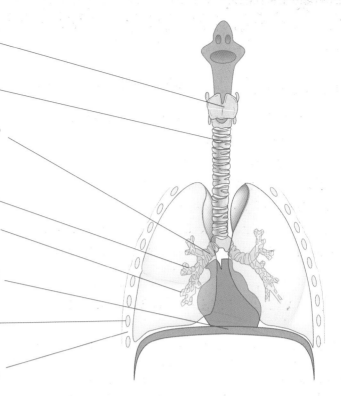

larynx – air passage to the bronchus; air passing over the larynx produces the voice

trachea (windpipe) – has rings of cartilage along its length to allow the tube to be flexible and to keep the airway open

bronchi – tubes that branch from the trachea to continue the air flow nearer to the lungs

bronchioles – smaller sub-divisions of the bronchi leading to the alveoli

alveoli – tiny air sacs; there are millions in the lungs; gaseous exchange takes place here; this action is vital to sustain life

diaphragm – sheet of muscle dividing the chest cavity and the abdominal cavity

ribs – form a protective cage around the organs in the chest

intercostal muscles – found between the ribs contracting and relaxing in the breathing process

What to do:

1. In your own words, write a description of the following parts of the body linked with the respiratory system: trachea, bronchi, bronchioles, lungs, alveoli, diaphragm, intercostal muscles and ribs.

2 Role of the Lungs

The lungs are positioned inside the chest cavity. The ribs form a cage protecting them. The right lung is bigger than the left lung. This is because it has three cavities and the left only has two.

The action of breathing means that the lungs are constantly moving in and out. To protect the lungs from any friction, due to the movement, the pleural membrane forms a complete lining around them. The pleural membrane is smooth and has a moist, slimy mucus.

From the nose or mouth, air enters the trachea and moves towards the lungs. It divides into two branches called the 'bronchi'. These subdivide into smaller tubes called 'bronchioles'. At the end of these are alveoli. These are air sacs with many mini blood vessels called 'capillaries' running from them.

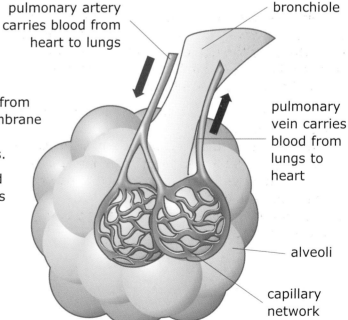

pulmonary artery carries blood from heart to lungs

bronchiole

pulmonary vein carries blood from lungs to heart

alveoli

capillary network

The millions of alveoli allow gases to exchange inside them. Here is a simplified version of what happens:

- Oxygen from the air breathed in enters the circulatory system to be used by the working muscles.
- Carbon dioxide, which is toxic or harmful to the system, transfers from the used blood, out of the circulatory system, back into the alveoli, to be breathed out.
- The capillaries, covering the surface of the alveoli, link the respiratory system with the circulatory system.

The exchange of gases is vital for our survival. With training, this exchange becomes more efficient as more alveoli are prepared to make the swap between oxygen (in) and carbon dioxide (out). Regular exercise conditions the lungs to excrete more of the poisonous carbon dioxide from the body. If too much carbon dioxide remained in the body, it would be fatal.

The lungs, at different stages of breathing, have varying amounts of air in them. **Tidal volume** is the amount of air breathed in and out of the body during normal breathing. During exercise, the volume is forced to change. Therefore, it is called '**forced breathing**'. **Vital capacity** is the largest amount or volume of air that can be exhaled (breathed out) after the largest possible inhalation (breath in). **Residual volume** is the amount of air that, even after as much air as possible has been exhaled, is left in the lungs.

What to do:

1. Using the previous page to help, write four sentences on key points about the lungs. Use the following words as headings:
   - Position
   - Protection
   - Exchange of gases
   - Effects of training

3 Mechanism of Breathing

Lungs are not muscle. Lungs cannot move of their own accord, nor are they controlled by the central nervous system. So, how do they move when we breathe in and out? The key to breathing is the diaphragm and the intercostal muscles between the ribs.

When we breathe in –
inspiration – the
following happens:

- our diaphragm pulls down
- our intercostal muscles contract
- air pressure is reduced
- air is sucked through the tubes into the lungs
- our chest expands.

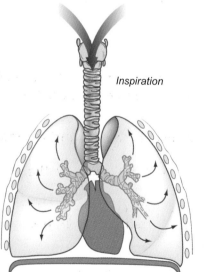

Inspiration

When we breathe out –
expiration – the opposite happens:

- our diaphragm relaxes into its dome position
- our intercostal muscles relax
- our chest becomes smaller
- pressure increases on our lungs
- air is forced out.

Expiration

What to do:

1. In your own words, describe the action of breathing.

Use the following words to help you: nose, mouth, trachea, lungs, ribs, intercostal muscles and diaphragm.

Task 2

Task 3

Behind the scenes

We can feel our chest expand and fall as we breathe in and out. What we are not aware of is the change in the air going into and out of our body. The air we breathe in is very different from the air that we breathe out. We now know why we breathe, so let's look at the changes in inhaled and exhaled air.

The parts that make up inhaled and exhaled air are called its 'composition'.

Composition of inhaled air

79% = nitrogen
20% = oxygen
trace = carbon dioxide

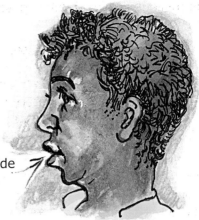

Composition of exhaled air

79% = nitrogen
16% = oxygen
4% = carbon dioxide

What to do:

1. Make a table showing the composition of inhaled and exhaled air.

●●●● ▶ Active Challenge

Exhaled air has more moisture in it. This is because water is a waste product. Some water is removed from your body as you breathe out. Moisture in exhaled air is demonstrated by the mirror test.

Hold a mirror just below your lower lip and exhale. What do you see?

When you are exercising, how else is water removed from the body?

The respiration and circulation link

There has to be a link between the respiratory and circulatory systems. The oxygen has to go from the respiratory system to the circulatory system and back to the respiratory system again. It follows this order:

- The oxygen breathed in goes through the mouth or nose, down the trachea, into the lungs and into the alveoli (air sacs).
- The oxygen passes through the alveoli walls into the red blood cells, via the capillaries.
- The oxygen joins with haemoglobin to make oxyhaemoglobin.
- The oxyhaemoglobin is used by the working body and is transported by the circulatory system to cells needing to release energy.
- Carbon dioxide is produced as a waste product.
- This is converted into a gas and passes back through the alveoli walls, via the capillaries into the blood plasma.
- Blood takes it back to the capillaries in the lungs.
- The carbon dioxide passes through the capillary and alveoli walls into the alveoli (air sacs).
- It is then exhaled from the body.

Alveoli	► air sacs where gaseous exchange takes place
Diaphragm	► muscle that divides the chest cavity from the abdominal cavity
Expiration	► breathing out, exhalation
Forced breathing	► breathing during exercise when requirements increase
Inspiration	► breathing in, inhalation
Residual volume	► the amount of air left in the lungs after a maximal exhalation
Tidal volume	► amount of air breathed in or out during normal breathing
Vital capacity	► amount of air that can be breathed out, after a deep breath in

4 How Exercise Affects Breathing

We have learned how important the action of breathing is. It puts oxygen into the body and removes carbon dioxide. At rest, we take an average of 15 breaths per minute. This is called the 'tidal volume'. This is enough breath for rest but when we start to exercise greater amounts of oxygen are needed and greater amounts of carbon dioxide are produced, which need to be removed. In extreme activity the breathing rate can go up to 50 breaths per minute.

The amount of oxygen a person is able to take up will increase. There is a limit to the increase in each person, which is called the 'VO$_2$ maximum'. During exercise, the vital capacity will increase because of the demand for greater intake of air. Both the residual volume and the tidal volume increase only slightly.

5 Aerobic and Anaerobic Activity

The body converts fuel to energy and releases it into the body through aerobic and anaerobic respiration. The systems automatically kick in depending on the type and intensity of the exercise performed.

Aerobic fitness

Energy released in aerobic activity needs a sufficient supply of oxygen to the tissues. With enough oxygen present the activity can go on for long periods, as long as the difficulty or intensity does not become too great. This aerobic fitness allows us to keep going at a moderate level. The aerobic system is used in moderate to hard continuous activities that usually take place over a period of more than 60 seconds. The oxygen is breathed in and diffused into the circulatory system. In this type of activity, breathing becomes more regular and deeper. The muscles need oxygen to contract and in aerobic respiration this oxygen enters the body by the breathing process.

Extra air = aerobic

The formula for this is:
glucose + oxygen ➜ carbon dioxide, water, energy

Long distance runners, such as Paula Radcliffe, need aerobic respiration.

Anaerobic fitness

When energy is produced anaerobically no oxygen is used in its initial release. Some sports wholly use anaerobic respiration. These are activities where there is a need for a single maximum burst of energy. Athletic field events are good examples of anaerobic exercise. In throwing and jumping events the actions used are explosive. They use one all-out burst of maximum effort to complete the event. The time it takes to complete the attempt is very short, so the energy is produced from the supplies already in the body.

The demand of the muscles for oxygen is so great that the cardiovascular systems do not have time to supply the demand. In anaerobic respiration the energy is provided not by oxygen but by adenosine triphosphate (ATP) and creatine phosphate (CP).

ATP and CP can only supply energy for a short time. If the demand for energy continues for over a minute then this releases energy by breaking down carbohydrates. This is called the '**lactic acid** system'. The side effect of the body using this system is that a build-up of lactic acid could occur in the muscles, which can lead to fatigue.

No air = anaerobic   The formula is:
glucose → carbon dioxide, water, energy, lactic acid

Athletic field events use anaerobic respiration, Steve Backley demonstrates this in the men's javelin.

You can tell when a player has just used their anaerobic system from their breathing pattern. After working very hard in the activity their breath may be shallow and gasping. This is an indication that there is an **oxygen debt**, a state in which the body needs more oxygen than it can supply.

This type of energy provision can only carry on for 45–60 seconds. After this, the lactic acid in the muscles becomes too high and prevents muscular contraction. The anaerobic system stops. The body then cannot keep running at its fastest speed or keep lifting heavy weights.

In all games, a combination of aerobic and anaerobic respiration is required. A player while moving and positioning themself correctly on the pitch according to the play is using aerobic respiration. This is aerobic because the intensity of the exercise is moderate and will continue throughout the game. When the player takes a shot, for example, one maximal contraction is used. For this action, the anaerobic system comes into operation.

A games player will use both aerobic and anaerobic respiration.

Squash players, for example, use both types of respiration. Footballers use anaerobic respiration more. This is due to the need for a maximal effort whenever they strike the ball during a rally.

What to do:

1. Study the comments below on the changes in respiration to an athlete in a sprint race. Put them into the order in which the athlete would experience them.

   a. The oxygen debt is repaid.

   b. She breathes quickly and respires aerobically.

   c. Her muscles ache.

   d. The lactic acid system begins to provide energy.

   e. She begins anaerobic respiration in her muscles.

   f. She breathes slowly and respires aerobically.

6 What Happens to the Body During Exercise and Why?

Oxygen inhaled regularly for aerobic respiration; tidal volume increases.

Air exhaled to stop the build-up of carbon dioxide.

Breathing rate increases and becomes deeper and more regular = aerobic respiration.

Heart beat increases, supplying the demand for more oxygen in the working muscles.

Stroke volume increases as the heart sends out more blood per beat.

Blood flow reduced to areas not in use, like the digestive system.

Fatigue in muscles, as ability to use oxygen for the production of energy becomes less efficient.

Blood moves to skin surface, helping heat loss.

Gaseous exchange in alveoli – with training the gaseous exchange becomes more efficient as more alveoli are prepared to take on the exchange of oxygen and carbon dioxide.

Waste water released from the body as sweat on surface of the skin.

Release of energy – glycogen is stored in muscles and the liver and released as glucose to allow the muscles to work.

Adrenaline (a hormone) released preparing the body for action.

The effects of exercise and the link between the circulatory and respiratory systems

What to do:

1. Make a list of the physical changes that happen to an athlete during exercise.

Long-term effects of training on the respiratory system

Correct training prepares the body in many ways. Endurance training makes the exchange of gases in the alveoli more efficient. The muscles are able to work at a moderate to hard level for longer without tiring. The effect this has on the body is to increase the vital capacity of the lungs. This means that more air is exhaled and so more carbon dioxide can leave the body in one breath and more air can be breathed in, getting more oxygen to the working muscles. Interval training over short distances at fast speeds results in an oxygen debt. By continuing this training new capillaries are formed, heart muscle is strengthened and the delivery of oxygen is improved, which stops the build-up of lactic acid. The overall effect is called an 'oxygen debt tolerance', which the performer develops through this type of training.

7 How the Body Recovers from Physical Activity

As the intensity of the exercise becomes less, the demand for oxygen to fuel the muscles also gets less. Breathing becomes less deep as a result. There are many differences in people which affect the time we take to recover from physical activity:

- time and intensity of the exercise
- physical differences of size and weight
- age
- sex
- fitness level.

 Active Challenge

Count the number of breaths you make at rest for one minute.

Perform maximal exercise, such as step-ups, for one minute.

Again, count the number of breaths for one minute.

Time how long it takes your breathing to return to resting rate.

Key Terms:

Lactic acid	► chemical built up in the muscles during anaerobic exercise
Oxygen debt	► shortfall of oxygen to the body after maximal effort/anaerobic exercise, resulting in deep and shallow breathing
Release of energy	► amount and type of energy release used at different stages in different kinds of an activity

Summary

A fit and healthy respiratory system is vital. It fuels the muscles and takes away poisonous carbon dioxide from the body. Aerobic and anaerobic systems are used at different times depending on the types of stress put on the body. The respiratory and circulatory systems are linked. The key is the link between the alveoli of the respiratory system and the capillaries of the circulatory system. Training improves the systems.

Bones

What you will learn about in this section

1. The Function of the Skeleton
2. The Names of Bones
3. How Bones Grow
4. Parts of a Fully Formed Bone
5. The Different Shapes of Bones
6. How Bones Are Grouped Together
7. What is the Function of Certain Bones?
8. How Bones Help the Sportsperson
9. Bones Linked With Sporting Actions

1 The Function of the Skeleton

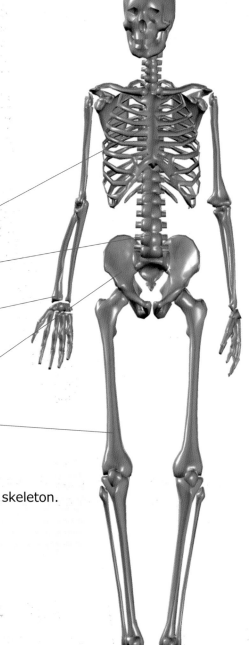

We take for granted having a **skeleton** but have you ever thought what we would be like without one? A mass of muscle and tissue on the floor is not a pretty sight. The bones of the skeleton have five important jobs to do. Some of these jobs are more obvious than others.

The skeleton gives us our general **shape** and determines whether we are tall or short, broad or narrow.

The bones of the skeleton **support** the rest of the body.

The skeleton helps the body to **move** by providing a framework onto which muscles attach.

Some bones help to **protect** the internal organs of the body.

What is not that obvious is that **production** of red and white blood cells takes place in some bones of the body.

What to do:

1. Using the above section, pick out the five different functions of the skeleton.
2. When you have found them, copy the spidergram below.
3. Put one function at the end of each line.

SKELETON

2 The Names of Bones

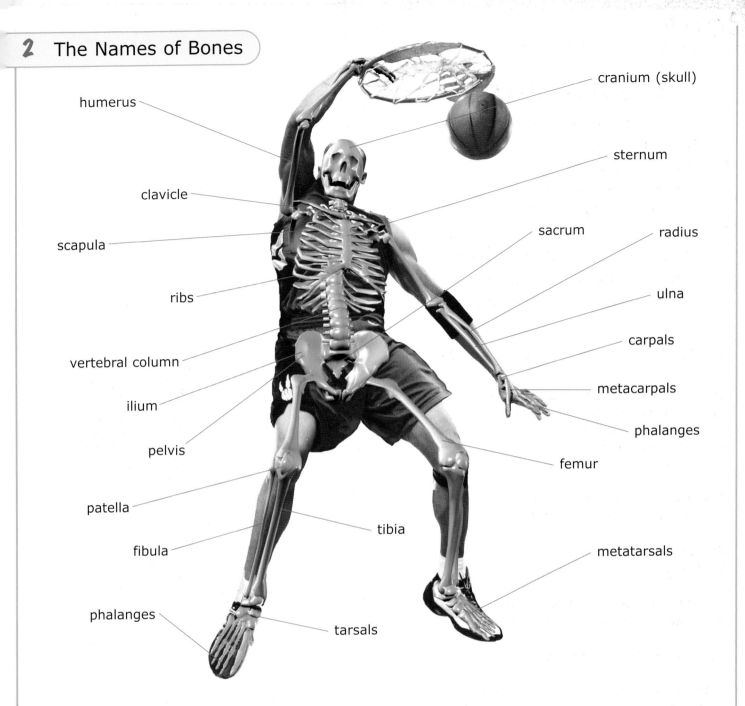

humerus

clavicle

scapula

ribs

vertebral column

ilium

pelvis

patella

fibula

phalanges

cranium (skull)

sternum

sacrum

radius

ulna

carpals

metacarpals

phalanges

femur

tibia

metatarsals

tarsals

What to do:

1. Learn the names of the bones in the body.
2. Start by trying to memorise the bones of the upper body.
3. When you feel confident go on to the bones of the lower body.

> Remember ulna is underneath the radius and the tibia is on top of the fibula.
>
> The phalanges are both fingers and toes!

●●●● ▶ Active Challenge

Take turns in testing your partner. Point to a bone in your body and see if your partner can tell you its name. Use the picture above only when you need to.

Functions of the bones

Shape

The way bones are arranged gives us our general framework and shape. When someone is said to be of a large build it is partly because of the size of their skeleton. Certain builds are more suited to particular sports. When you look at different sportspeople you will be able to work out their general shape and size of skeleton. Jockeys have a skeleton that is likely to be small and thin, a basketball player is often long and thin.

Support

As bones are firm and rigid they can support the rest of the body and keep us upright. Part of the body is made up of muscle, which is held in place by being attached to the skeleton. The bones act as an anchor or framework upon which the rest of the body tissues, like muscles, can hang.

Help with movement

When the bones work with the muscles of the body they allow the body to move. The skeleton provides a series of 'anchor points' to which the muscles attach. When bones are made to work by muscles they work as levers and so allow a variety of movements in everyday life and when we play sports. When a sportsperson swings a racket to hit a tennis ball for instance, the **long bones** of the arm help create the leverage necessary to apply force to the shot.

Protection

Some bones help to protect the internal organs of the body. These are the bones and arrangements of bone that enclose other parts of the body. They act a little like a box. This is especially important to the sportsperson playing contact sports or team games. A volleyball player dives to make a dig, a footballer heads a ball and a rugby player takes a tackle. The vital organs of the body would not last long if they did not have certain bones to protect them. Examples of these protecting bones are: skull, pelvis, rib cage and vertebrae.

What to do:

1. Use skull, pelvis, rib cage and vertebrae as headings.
2. List underneath each of these headings the part of the body they protect.
3. Use the word bank below to help you.
4. Each word links with only one set of the protecting bones.

Word bank

brain   **spinal cord**   **heart**   **lungs**   **spleen**   **stomach**   **bladder**   **liver**

Task 3

Applied Anatomy and Physiology

Production of blood cells

In the **long bones** of the body, the production of red and white blood cells takes place. As blood cells keep wearing out it is important that new supplies are made. The job of white blood cells is to go to any source of infection to fight germs and bacteria. Cells need to be regenerating constantly so the body can be guarded from disease. Red blood cells transport oxygen from the lungs to the rest of the body.

What to do:

1. Copy and complete the sentences below about each function of the skeleton.

   a. Some people choose a particular sport because of their _____ owing to their skeleton size.

   b. Red blood cells are constantly being _____ in the long bones of the skeleton.

   c. We need our skeleton to work with the muscles to allow different _____.

   d. The skeleton provides the _____ upon which muscles can hang.

   e. When a player heads a ball their brain is _____ by part of their skeleton.

Key Terms:

Long bones	► those bones that are the longest in the body which make up the arms and legs
Move	► a motion, could be an action like running or swinging a racket at a ball
Production	► making something
Protect	► guard against threat of injury
Shape	► form or outline
Skeleton	► the arrangement of the 206 bones of the human body
Support	► helping to take the weight

3 How Bones Grow

There are certain times in a person's life when their bones develop. The four main stages of bone development are:

- pre-natal (before birth)
- newly born
- childhood
- puberty.

Bones take many years to develop fully, but all bone development begins in one of two ways. Most bones start as **cartilage** and then undergo a series of processes to give them a much firmer structure.

In adulthood most people reach their peak and are strong, fast and can compete at their best. This applies especially to team games.

In ladies gymnastics the flexibility still allowed by a young girl is vital to the success of a performance. Russia's Yulia Barsukova won a gold medal for her performance at the 2000 Olympics.

Task 4

Active Challenge

To give you an idea of what cartilage feels like, pinch your nose just below the bridge (hard part) and move your hand from side to side. You will find that it is moveable. This is cartilage.

What to do:

1. Make a list of the four main times when bone development occurs.

2. Write down why it is important that bone develops and becomes harder.

Growth and development of bones

The name for the growth and development of bones is **ossification**. This process begins in the embryo and continues through puberty until the late teens.

Long bones are formed in a systematic and progressive manner. Firstly, when the long bone achieves its general shape it is cartilage. This cartilage model will keep its general shape throughout development. A fine tissue layer then develops around the bone along its shaft. This **periosteal collar** will appear around the **shaft** of the cartilage model.

The cartilage then takes on a big transformation. It begins to **calcify**. The model begins to change. The cartilage cells begin to die off as they are replaced with calcified tissue. When they die they leave spaces and so the area becomes like a honeycomb. The gaps that are left are filled with bone-forming cells called **osteoblasts**, blood vessels and **osteoclasts** (bone-eroding cells). The osteoblasts, blood vessels and osteoclasts are arranged in irregular layers in the cartilage model.

The process begins in the **diaphysis** (long part of the bone) but then extends into the ends of the bones (**epiphyses**). This gives three areas where ossification takes place.

What to do:

1. Read the section above about ossification.

2. Rearrange the statements below into a logical order of when they occur in the body.

   a. Cartilage cells die and leave spaces.

   b. The periosteal collar appears where there is no cartilage.

   c. Osteoblasts, blood vessels and osteoclasts are arranged in irregular layers.

   d. Long bones start their development as a cartilage model.

   e. Ossification extends along the shaft to the ends of the bone.

   f. The cartilage in the shaft of the bone calcifies.

   g. Ossification occurs in three parts of the bone: the shaft and at either end.

   h. The gaps left when the cartilage dies are filled with osteoblasts, blood vessels and osteoclasts.

The development of bones

Long bone development

Long bones start as a cartilage model and keep this general shape during development.

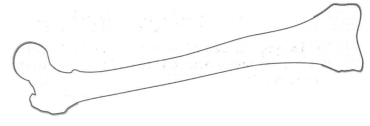

Then the periosteal collar appears, which is a strong fibrous cover on the shaft of the bone.

Periosteal collar forms

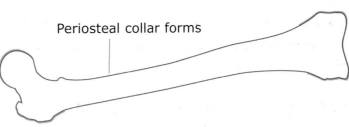

Cartilage in the shaft of the bone becomes calcified. At each end of the calcified area bone growth takes place.

bone becomes calcified

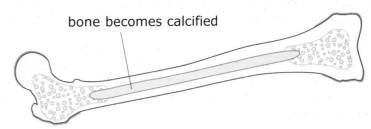

Cartilage dies off and so leaves gaps. The structure becomes honeycombed.

cartilage dies off, leaving gaps

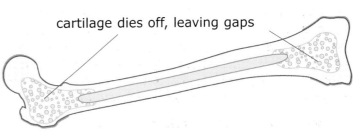

The gaps are filled with:

- osteoblasts
- blood vessels
- osteoclasts.

This area is made of spongy bone.

gaps filled with osteoblasts, blood vessels and osteoclasts

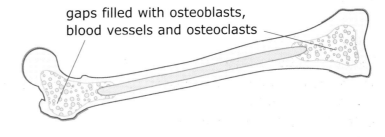

As development continues there are three centres of ossification: in the diaphysis and the epiphyses. The bone contains red blood cells. Under the periosteum are bone-forming cells/osteoblasts.

diaphysis

epiphysis

epiphysis

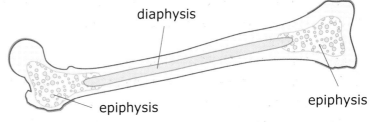

What to do:

1. Copy the above drawings into your book.
2. Give each of the diagrams a heading that fits what happens at that stage of development.
3. Write down the main ideas relating to bone development.

Task 7

4 Parts of a Fully Formed Bone

The parts of a fully formed bone are described below.

- Bone is still covered by the periosteal collar.
- This is a thin layer of tissue made up of many fibres.
- It is this covering that contains blood cells.
- On the inside of this surface the bone-forming cells are to be found.
- These osteoblasts have the capability of making repairs to the bone after injury.
- The ends of the bones are called the epiphyses and are spongy bone.
- Another name for spongy bone is **cancellous bone**.
- The shaft, under the periosteum, is a layer of **compact bone**.
- **Yellow bone marrow** fills the centre of the bone shaft.
- The diaphysis makes up the length of the bone.

What to do:

1. Use the statements above as your guide.
2. Copy and label this picture of a fully developed long bone (the femur).

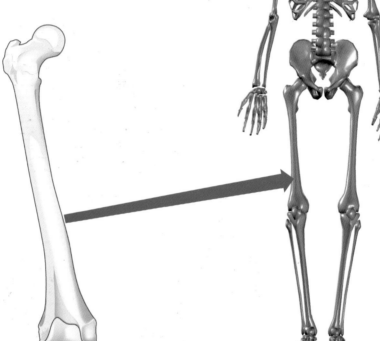

Key Terms:

Calcify	▶ harden
Cancellous bone	▶ name for spongy bone; has air pockets so it looks like a sponge
Cartilage	▶ gristly tissue
Compact bone	▶ strong, hard bone
Diaphysis	▶ shaft of a long bone
Epiphysis	▶ end of a long bone
Ossification	▶ the development from cartilage to bone
Osteoblasts	▶ bone-forming cells
Osteoclasts	▶ bone-eroding cells
Periosteal collar/periosteum	▶ membrane surrounding the shaft of a bone
Shaft	▶ long, thin part of a long bone
Yellow bone marrow	▶ substance found in the shaft of a long bone

Applied Anatomy and Physiology

5 The Different Shapes of Bones

There are four different **classifications** of bones. We have already read and learned about long bones. The other types are **short**, **flat** and **irregular** bones. The way differently shaped bones are arranged in the body allows them to perform certain jobs. It would be hard to imagine an irregular bone, like the pelvis, at the point between the elbow and the shoulder and being as efficient there as the long bone of the humerus. The role that the bone has to perform determines the shape, size and density (compactness) that it is.

Long bones

humerus ⎤
radius   ⎬── arm
ulna   ⎦

femur ⎤
tibia ⎬── leg
fibula ⎦

metacarpals ⎤
phalanges   ⎬── hands and feet
metatarsals ⎦

Short bones

carpals ── hands

tarsals ── feet

Irregular bones

vertebrae
patella
jawbone
cheekbone

Flat (plate) bones

cranium
clavicle
scapula
sternum
ribs
pelvis

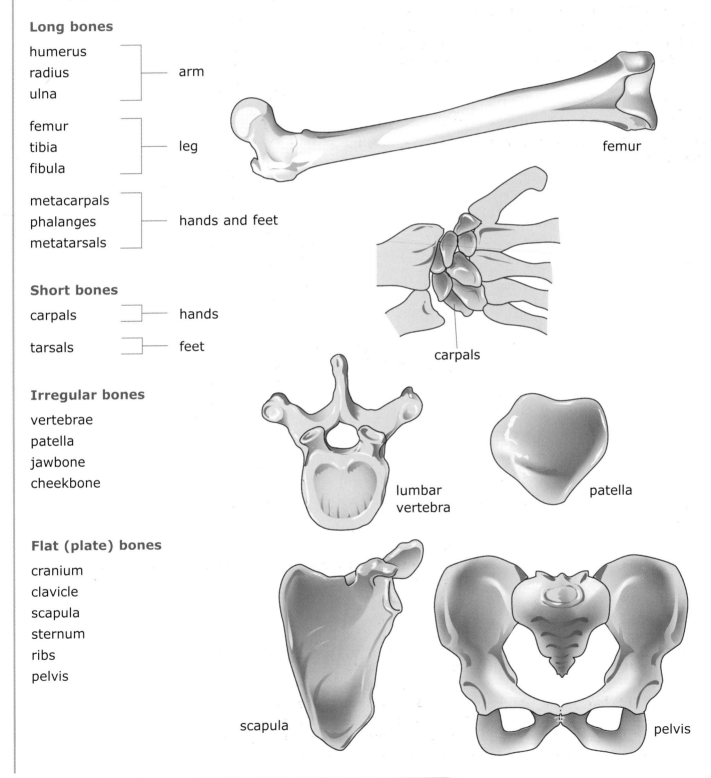

femur

carpals

lumbar
vertebra

patella

scapula

pelvis

Task 9

What to do:

1. Make a list of all the bones in the following groups:
   a. irregular
   b. flat
   c. long
   d. short.

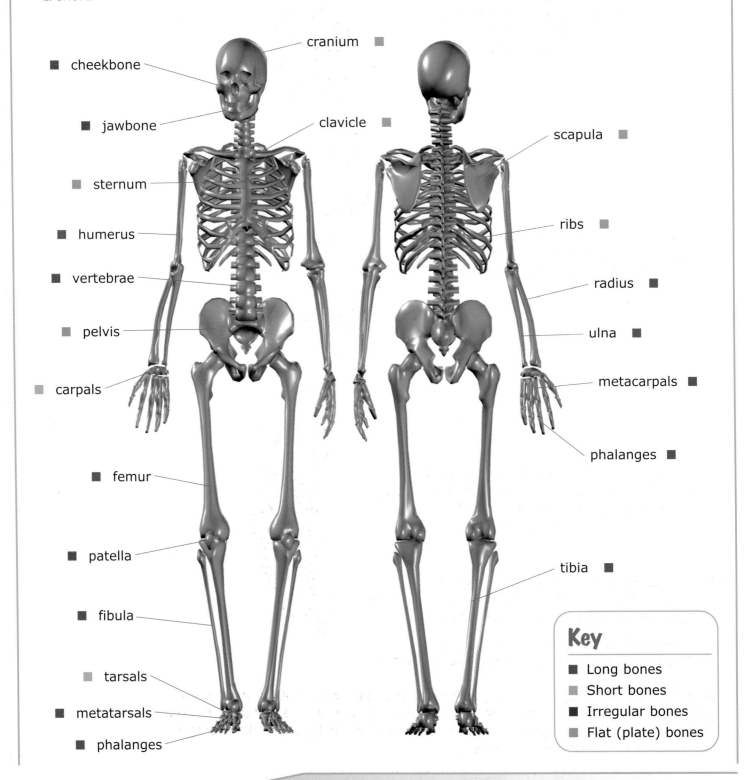

cheekbone ■

jawbone ■

sternum ▨

humerus ■

vertebrae ■

pelvis ▨

carpals ▨

femur ■

patella ■

fibula ■

tarsals ▨

metatarsals ■

phalanges ■

cranium ▨

clavicle ▨

scapula ▨

ribs ▨

radius ■

ulna ■

metacarpals ■

phalanges ■

tibia ■

Key

■ Long bones

▨ Short bones

■ Irregular bones

▨ Flat (plate) bones

Applied Anatomy and Physiology

The vertebrae

The **vertebrae** are irregular bones. There are 33 of these bones making the vertebral column. They are placed in five groups according to where they are along the vertebral column.

- **Cervical** vertebrae allow different movements at the top of the spine; there are seven of them. The top two vertebrae, the atlas and the axis, allow you to nod and turn your head

- The **thoracic** region has 12 vertebrae. Ten of these are attached to the ribs and help movement when breathing.

- The five **lumbar** vertebrae are the most robust as they take a lot of weight. They are also large because they are in the area that allows the most movement.

- The **sacrum** has five vertebrae, which become fused together in adulthood. They make up part of the pelvic girdle.

- At the end of the spine is the **coccyx**. There are four vertebrae here, all fused together.

All the vertebrae fit together neatly to protect the spinal cord. This is an important job as any damage to the cord can be paralysing. In between the vertebrae there are cartilage discs. These help stop damage, wear and tear, and grinding down of the vertebrae through constant movement.

8 How Bones Help the Sportsperson

Long bones, due to their length, create **leverage** when playing sport. Whether hitting a shuttlecock or bowling a ball, long bones play an important role in the performance of the player, helping to generate speed, force and power.

Flat bones are tough and can withstand hard impact. The cranium takes a hard blow when heading a ball. When a rugby player is in a tackle his pelvis and rib cage can protect his internal organs owing to their strength.

Short bones are specialists for fine movements, especially those of the hand. Short bones are responsible for putting spin on a ball in cricket and rounders, and for helping a ball accurately hit a target. As these bones can make small adjustments they help keep the body balanced – important for the gymnast and golfer.

Bones have different uses depending on where they are in the body. Some, like the vertebrae, work together and act as a shock absorber. When players land on their feet from a jump it is the vertebrae that help reduce the shock on their backs.

9 Bones Linked With Sporting Actions

Whenever a sportsperson is in action, they are relying on their skeleton to play a supporting role in their performance; bones are also designed to help the action. Whatever a sportsperson does, bones are there, helping them to move efficiently.

- When a bowler spins a cricket ball they are relying on the bones of their hand to help apply the spin, so the carpals, metacarpals and phalanges are important.
- Swinging a racket to play a forehand drive in tennis involves the bones of the arm. Therefore the scapula, humerus, radius and ulna help the swing action of the stroke.
- Landing on their feet after playing a spike or smash, volleyball players require their legs to cushion the landing. Here the pelvis at the hip, the femur, patella, tibia and fibula in the legs, plus the tarsals, metatarsals and phalanges in the feet, are in play to make the landing safe and the body balanced and ready for the next movement.

 **Active Challenge**

Work with a partner. Point to different bones and ask your partner to say what class of bone they are. Take turns to link a sporting movement with the class of bone indicated.

There are two levels to this task. Choose **one** of them to complete.

What to do:

Level 1 Give one example of each bone type and link it with a sporting action.
Level 2 Give two examples of each bone type and link them with a sporting action. Use common names and proper names when describing areas of the body. For example, irregular bone, in the lower back – lumbar vertebrae – bending to field a ball in rounders.

> Choose a bone type and say where it is located in the body. Give the name of the bone and explain the sporting action that uses it. Put them together and that is your answer.

What to do:

1. Look carefully at the pictures on the next page of people playing different sports.
2. Work out the action that they are performing and name the bones involved.
3. Write a heading for each action that you see and give the names of the bones that are involved in the specific action.

Sporting actions use various bones for movement.

Key Terms:

Cervical	► bones of the vertebrae forming the neck
Classification	► a way of sorting or organising groups
Coccyx	► bones of the vertebrae, fused at the extreme lower end of the vertebral column
Flat bone	► can be called plate bone, mainly linked with protection
Irregular bones	► bones that have no uniform shape
Leverage	► the use of force or effort (muscle power) to overcome resistance
Lumbar	► bones of the vertebrae in the lower back region
Sacrum	► bones of the vertebrae, fused in adults, making part of the pelvic girdle
Short bone	► smaller version of a long bone, found in the hands and feet
Thoracic	► bones of the vertebrae in the chest area
Vertebrae	► irregular bones that run the length of the body from head to rear

Summary

Bones perform seen and unseen functions. A person may choose a sport because their body shape suits that particular activity and so they can be successful. The sportsperson relies on the strength of bones to withstand pressure and knocks in contact sports and so bones protect vital organs of the body. A shot to beat a keeper or a passing shot in tennis needs the length of the long bones to bring leverage to the action. The long bones help movements to be powerful and forceful.

Athletes need their small bones to aid in small movements, such as in balance and agility, important when dodging around the opposition or changing direction in a gymnastic movement. The skeleton supports the muscles. It is this anchoring that enables the muscles to work and bring about movement. Production of red and white blood cells occurs in some bones of the body. This is essential so that the body can function, as the cells transport oxygen and nutrients, and fight infection.

Joints

What you will learn about in this section

1. The Definition of a Joint
2. Different Joint Locations in the Body
3. The Significance of Synovial Joints
4. In-depth Understanding of Synovial Joints
5. Functions of Different Parts of a Joint
6. The Importance of Cartilage, Tendons and Ligaments in Sport
7. Different Types of Synovial Joint
8. The Range of Movement at Joints
9. Effects of Age on Flexibility of the Joints
10. How Joints Help the Sportsperson

1 The Definition of a Joint

> A **joint** is the place where two or more bones meet.
>
> There does not have to be movement there.

The **fused** bones of the cranium are as much a joint as the meeting of the humerus and ulna at the elbow. The joints where there is movement are more significant to the actions of the sportsperson.

Some joints allow a large range of movements, such as the hip joint. Other joints, like the joint at the wrist, give much smaller and more restricted movement. This is owing to the size and arrangement of the bones. Although there are elements common to all joints, each type is formed in a different way and it is this arrangement that leads to the different ways we can move.

What to do:

1. Write out a definition of the word 'joint'.

Skiing involves a range of movements at different joints.

Task 1

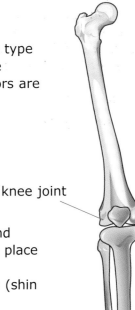

2 Different Joint Locations in the Body

The following are all **synovial** joints. These joints allow the greatest movement. You only need to remember those in bold.

What to do:

1. Make a table of the body's joints.
2. State where the joints are in the body. Use neck, knee, hip, elbow and shoulder as headings.
3. State the type of joint each is and the bones involved.

neck (**pivot**)

cranium (fixed)

shoulder (**ball and socket**)

sacroiliac (a joint at the back of the pelvis – helps absorb the shock of landing on feet)

hip (**ball and socket**)

coccyx (fixed)

elbow (**hinge**)

wrist (condyloid)

ankle (hinge and gliding)

knee (**hinge**)

3 The Significance of Synovial Joints

Freely moveable joints are common in the human body. The components of this type of joint have built-in safety factors to help guard against injury. These joints are designed to reduce wear and tear, absorb shock and reduce friction. These factors are especially important when performing skills at pace and with power.

4 In-depth Understanding of Synovial Joints

Knee joint

knee joint

There are many parts to the knee joint. Its position demands that it can withstand hard pressure. This makes it a robust joint. The ligaments that hold the bones in place are called the 'cruciates'. When footballers have serious knee injuries it is these ligaments that are often damaged. Between the femur (thigh bone) and the tibia (shin bone) is the semi-lunar **cartilage** that helps lubricate the joint. This is also the damaged or torn tissue in knee twisting injuries and cartilage problems.

What to do:

1. Copy the diagram of a knee joint.
2. Refer to work already studied on the skeleton and then label your diagram.

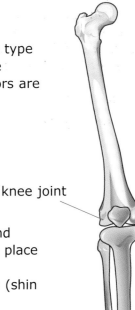

Task 2

Task 3

Cartilage covers the ends of the bones where they meet and stops the bones touching each other. This is called 'hyaline cartilage'. The cartilage acts as a cushion and creates a barrier reducing the amount of **friction** that occurs when the bones are moving against each other. This stops the bones wearing each other away.

Synovial fluid lubricates the joint, like oiling the chain of a bike or putting oil in a car, allowing all the parts to move against each other smoothly. Synovial fluid works in the same way. It also keeps the joint free from infection.

Synovial membrane lies inside the capsule. It is here that the synovial fluid is produced.

Synovial capsule is a tough fibre that surrounds the joint, holding the fluid in place.

Ligaments surround the sides of the joint. Ligaments are made of tough elastic fibres. It is the ligaments that hold the bones in place, thus keeping the joint together. The stability of the joint relies on the strength of the ligaments and on the muscles supporting the joint.

Tendons are not strictly part of the joint, although they play an important part in the joint's movement. Their job is to attach muscle to bone. Without tendons muscle would float around the bone and movement would be impossible. It is this attachment that creates an anchor for muscles to shorten and bring about different actions. Tendons are very strong because great exertion is required for some actions. As the muscle needs to be held firmly, the tendons act as a non-elastic anchor.

What to do:

1. Link the matching words. Each word can be used only once.

elastic   hyaline   lubricate

barrier between the bones   synovial fluid

reduces friction   tough fibre   ligaments

stabilise   tough   acts as a cushion

attach bone to bone   helps move freely

synovial capsule   cartilage

surrounds the joint

> There are four groups to make. Use the above paragraphs to find the links.

Key Terms:

Cartilage	► tough, flexible tissue, can be found at the end of bones
Friction	► action of two surfaces rubbing together creating heat
Fused	► two or more bones knitted together so no movement occurs
Joint	► the point where two or more bones meet
Ligament	► tough, rounded, elastic fibre attaching bone to bone at a joint
Synovial capsule	► tough fibre surrounding the synovial joint
Synovial fluid	► fluid; found in synovial joint
Synovial joints	► freely moveable joints with ends covered in cartilage
Synovial membrane	► lining inside joint capsule where synovial fluid is produced
Tendons	► strong, non-elastic tissue attaching bone to muscle

Task 4

Cartilage is a shock absorber. When running, the knee takes a lot of pounding. It is the cartilage that acts as a cushion so that the bones do not rub together and wear away. If the cartilage were not there, pain would occur at the joint due to the friction of the bones rubbing together. This is especially important in activities like long distance running, where there is continued use of the joint. Cartilage damage is common in sportspeople. A frayed cartilage decreases the efficiency of the joint and is extremely painful too.

Ligaments attach bone to bone. As there is much movement of bones, ligaments have to be strong and elastic. If there were no ligaments the joint would be unstable. Running, stopping and changing direction all put pressure on the joint. When changing direction at speed it is the ligaments that keep the bones in the right place. If the ligaments are stretched too far then they tear and the joint **dislocates**. After tearing it is unlikely that the ligaments will return to their former strength.

Tendons attach muscle to bone. Without tendons muscle would float around the bone and movement would be impossible. It is this attachment that creates an anchor for muscles to shorten and bring about different actions. Great exertion is required for some actions, therefore tendons are strong and non-elastic. If a muscle is large or pulls in more than one direction more than one tendon may be needed to anchor it. A weightlifter moving a maximum weight needs their tendons to hold firm and keep still. That is why they are non-elastic, just like a pole-vaulter pulling on the pole after take off in order to clear the bar.

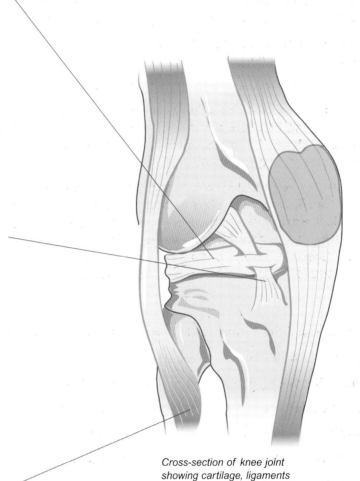

Cross-section of knee joint showing cartilage, ligaments and tendons.

What to do:

1. Write out three differences between cartilage, tendons and ligaments.

Task 5

There are different types of joint at varying places on the skeleton. Each type is distinguished by the variety of movement it allows, its size and the number of bones at the point of the joint.

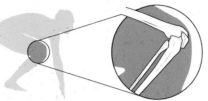

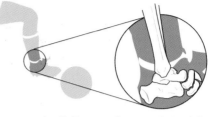

Knee/hinge – movement in two planes forwards and backwards with a small amount of rotation: running, kicking a football, sprint start position in swimming.

Ankle/hinge and gliding – forward and backward and some sideways and rotation: kicking a ball.

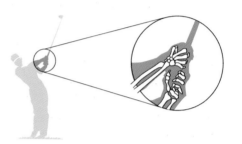

Neck/pivot – rotating and tilting the head: looking for ball, heading a ball.

Wrist/condyloid or gliding – forward and backward with some sideways movement: golfer will 'break' their wrists in the back swing

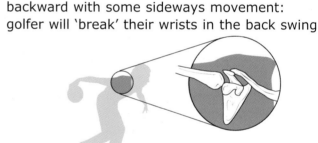

Elbow/hinge – movement in two planes forwards and backwards with a small amount of rotation: preparing to perform a chest pass, breaststroke arm action.

Shoulder/ball and socket – full rotation, allows the greatest amount of movement: arm action in front crawl, tennis serve action, bowling a ball.

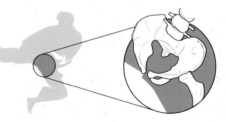

Fingers/hinge – in two directions forward and backwards gripping a racket.

Hip/ball and socket – rotation, allows a lot of movement: breaststroke leg action, trapping a ball on the inner thigh and bringing it down in football, performing a kick in karate.

What to do:

1. Describe how the following type of joints are used in particular sporting actions:
   a. ball and socket   b. hinge
   c. pivot.

If the centre of the body is where all movement comes from, then working out the different types of movement becomes simpler.

Adduction – this movement brings part of the body towards the centre. In the butterfly arm action, adduction is when the arms pull to the sides in the 's' shape. **Add**uction is **add**ing it to the body.

Abduction – this is the opposite action to adduction. The limbs are abducted from the centre. A goalkeeper abducts their arms when reaching to make a save. A badminton player abducts their arm when preparing for an overhead clear. A way to remember this is that when someone is kidnapped, they are abducted i.e. taken away.

Flexion – closing the angle at a joint. When preparing to throw a ball the angle at the elbow decreases. This movement of flexion gives the arm space to create power in the throw. Catching a ball and bringing it to the body is flexion at the wrist, elbow and shoulder joints. Recovery phase of the sprint leg action is flexion at the knee.

Extension – this is the opposite of flexion. It is when the angle increases between the bones at a joint. In the run up for a jump a long jumper takes off and extends the take off leg to generate as much upward lift as possible. This is an example of extension at the hips. Striding the leg forward to take a pace is extension at the knee.

Rotation – the angles do not change but the joint moves in a circular motion. The throwing action of the service in tennis, or the bowling action in cricket or rounders demonstrates this type of movement.

James Hickman on his way to winning the men's 400m medley demonstrates adduction of the arms, as he brings his arms back to his torso.

Abduction of the arms happens as Martin Pieckenhagen reaches to save the ball.

Harbhajan Singh shows how flexion occurs as the angle at the joint of both elbows decrease, in preparation to throw.

As Yann Domenech's right leg pushes back during take off, it extends.

Australian Lleyton Hewitt using a rotation movement to serve.

What to do:

1. Order the following joints from the greatest amount of movement to the least:

   hip

   shoulder

   knee

   elbow

   neck

2. Give your own example of a sporting movement for each.

3. Give the correct joint type.

Active Challenge

Point to a joint on your own body for your partner to tell you:
- the name of the joint
- what movement happens there
- the type of joint
- an example of the joints' use in sport.

9   Effects of Age on Flexibility of the Joints

At different ages the body is capable of different movements. When the young gymnast performing on the asymmetric bars changes her grip from overhand to underhand to swing around the bar, she dislocates her shoulders. This relies on the **flexibility** and the softness of the tissues at the joint. As performers get older tissues become less elastic and therefore their joints become less flexible and incapable of such adaptability. A warm-up that may have taken 15 minutes for a young teenager, may take 30 minutes when they are in their early twenties.

If practised in the correct way, flexibility can be increased. To achieve the same standards becomes harder as a person gets older. The less flexible a person is, the more prone to injury they are. The joints will be unable to withstand the shock of forceful contact with the ground. The amount of muscle strength reduces with age, which can lead to instability around joints and a lack of mobility. Later in life arthritis can begin. There is some evidence that arthritis is hereditary. It can also come about because of the rigours of a strenuous sporting life.

10   How Joints Help the Sportsperson

Joints work with muscles to create all movements in daily life and to complete sporting challenges. From the large strides of a long jumper to the small adjustments of the gymnast on the beam, it is joints that allow the range of movement seen. The agility required to dodge around an opponent and keep upright requires many frequent and minor adjustments from the tarsals, metatarsals and phalanges of the feet where they flex and extend to keep balanced. Striding, landing and taking weight could damage the bones if it were not for the cartilage that sits between them absorbing the shock.

In order that joints can achieve their full range they have to be prepared, trained and movements practised. To rotate the arm in the delivery of a javelin throw, a thorough warm-up is necessary, as well as all the previous training and conditioning. These make the joints more flexible, allowing a greater reach in the preparation and follow-through phases of a throw. The extra range leads to more leverage and the possibility of achieving a greater distance.

The sacroiliac joint, at the pelvis, is also a synovial joint. When a player makes a landing from a jump or a vault this joint at the pelvis is able to give, because it is a synovial joint. There is cartilage between the sacrum and the ilium. The movement allowed is crucial so that damage of such weight bearing movements keeps the joint uninjured.

Cartilaginous joints are joints in which the bones are attached by cartilage, such as the spinal column. Each vertebra sits on top of another and they are divided by cartilage. The cartilage prevents the bone from rubbing against another, wearing the bone down and resulting in pain. Cartilaginous joints do not have a joint capsule and synovial membrane like synovial joints.

Active Challenge

Work with a partner. Name a sporting action and ask your partner to link it with a joint, movement and sport.

Example
Kicking a football = knee = hinge joint = lower leg moves forward to straighten the leg after contact = extension.

What to do:

1. Link types of movement, joints and sporting actions together.

   Example of types of movement:
   - swimmer performing front crawl arm action
   - arm action required when shooting in netball or basketball.

Key Terms:

Abduction	▶ moving a limb or bone away from the body
Adduction	▶ moving a limb or bone towards the body
Dislocate	▶ move bones out of their usual joint arrangement
Extension	▶ increasing the angle at a joint
Flexibility	▶ a joint's ability to move through its full range
Flexion	▶ decreasing the angle at a joint
Rotation	▶ bone movement in a circular or part circular direction

Summary

A joint is a meeting of two or more bones. There may or may not be movement there. The synovial type of joint is the most important to the sportsperson as the different types give the range of movements to complete all sporting actions.

It is the different sizes of bones and the way in which they are arranged that give them their joint type.

In synovial joints there are parts that specialise in helping prevent injury and ensuring smooth action at the joint. These include cartilage, synovial fluid and ligaments. The sportsperson can perform all the movements required for success as long as each joint is kept healthy and strong.

Muscles

What you will learn about in this section

1. Three Kinds of Muscle
2. Location and Functions of Major Muscles
3. Link Muscles to Sporting Actions
4. Muscles' Relation to Bone
5. How Muscles Work in Pairs
6. Fast and Slow Twitch Muscle Fibres
7. Muscle Tone and Posture
8. Effect of Training on Muscles

1 Three Kinds of Muscle

Voluntary muscles, also known as skeletal or striated muscles, are the most common muscle-type in the body. These muscles attach to the skeleton and provide a person's shape. We can consciously control these muscles and dictate how their movement. Their movement happens like this:

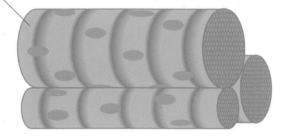

- A defender sees an attacker moving into a space.
- A message goes through the defender's nervous system to the brain.
- A decision is made through experience and training as to which muscles will be used in order to mark the opposition.
- The brain sends messages to the appropriate muscles.
- The action takes place.

All of this happens in a fraction of a second and this demonstrates why an attacker has a slight advantage over a defender. The defender can compensate for this by learning to read the game and prepare for the most likely course of action from the attacker.

Involuntary muscles, also known as smooth muscles, are not controlled; they work automatically. They carry on functioning throughout life. They are found in the intestines, blood vessels and urinary organs.

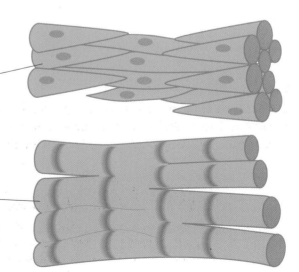

Cardiac muscle is a type of involuntary muscle, as it is not controlled consciously but works automatically. It is special because it is found only in the heart and it never rests during life.

What to do:

1. Using the headings **voluntary**, **involuntary** and **cardiac**, put the following words in the correct group:

automatic   striated   involuntary   never rests   controlled
intestines   heart   automatic   most common
smooth   blood vessels   consciously

2 Location and Functions of Major Muscles

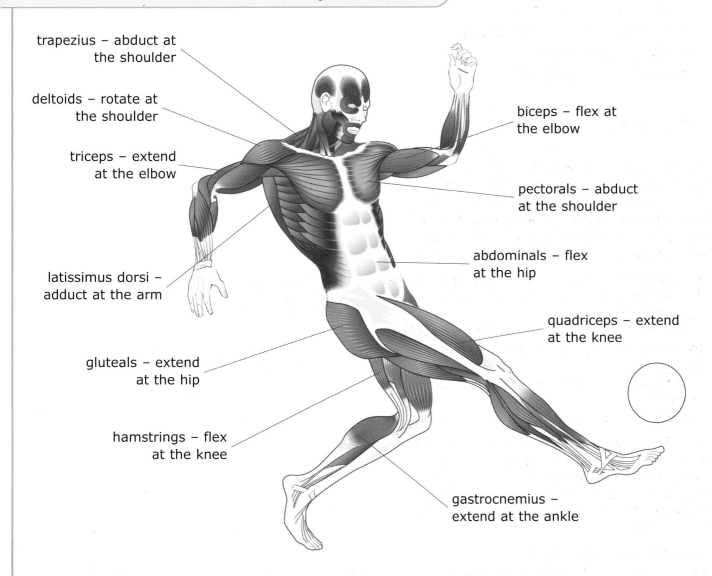

trapezius – abduct at the shoulder

deltoids – rotate at the shoulder

triceps – extend at the elbow

latissimus dorsi – adduct at the arm

gluteals – extend at the hip

hamstrings – flex at the knee

biceps – flex at the elbow

pectorals – abduct at the shoulder

abdominals – flex at the hip

quadriceps – extend at the knee

gastrocnemius – extend at the ankle

What to do:

1. Learn the names of the muscles of the body. Start by trying to memorise the muscles of the upper body. When you feel confident go on to the muscles of the lower body.

> Link the muscles with a bone you already know, this may help you to remember them.

●●●● ▶ **Active Challenge**

Work with a partner and take turns testing each other. Point to a muscle in your body and see if your partner can tell you its name. There are 11 types of muscle to remember.

3 Link Muscles to Sporting Actions

Voluntary muscle (also called skeletal muscle) is the type that flexes when performing a sporting action, such as pulling quads to extend at the knee to kick a ball.

What to do:

1. Use all of the muscles listed below.
2. Link them with a sporting action.
3. Use the sporting example on the previous page to help you.

   biceps, triceps, deltoids, pectorals, trapezius, abdominals, latissimus dorsi, gluteals, quadriceps, hamstrings, gastrocnemius

Example:
Abdominals, raise knee so flexing at the hips, used prior to take off in high jump.

4 Muscles' Relation to Bone

Voluntary muscle is attached to the bone by tendons. The muscle, at the point where it moves, is the **insertion** and the point where it is fixed is the **origin**. When the arm flexes at the elbow the movement is at the elbow, so the fixed point in this example is the shoulder.

The origins are the triceps and biceps at the shoulder.

The insertions are the triceps and biceps at the elbow.

Applied Anatomy and Physiology

What to do:

1. Copy the picture of an arm (on the previous page), showing the muscles clearly.
2. Label all the parts clearly.
3. Add in the origin and insertion of the muscle in another colour.

Key Terms:

Cardiac muscle	► only found in the heart, never tires
Insertion	► the point where a tendon attaches a muscle to bone where there is movement
Involuntary muscles	► work automatically, controlled by the involuntary nervous system
Origin	► the end of a muscle that is attached to a fixed bone
Voluntary muscles	► skeletal muscles attached to the skeleton, can be made to work consciously

5   How Muscles Work in Pairs

The body is moved by muscle groups, not by individual muscles. Muscles work in pairs. Muscles can only pull, therefore they need to work in partnership so movement can occur. The pulling muscle is called the **prime mover** (agonist). When a muscle pulls, it contracts or becomes shorter. The muscle relaxing is the **antagonist**. When a muscle relaxes it lengthens.

What to do:

1. In your own words, describe how muscles work in pairs.

Muscles work in pairs. Here, the quadriceps and hamstrings are working

There are two different types of fibre in muscles. There are **fast twitch muscle fibres** (FTMF) and **slow twitch muscle fibres** (STMF). Each type is better suited to different activities. Every person has a natural combination of both in their body. This amount cannot be changed, although with the correct training improvements can be made to the efficiency of each type. Games and racket sport players will have a fairly even distribution but some will have a higher percentage of fast twitch muscle fibres.

Fast twitch muscle fibres

When the nervous system decides an event requires short bursts of energy, the fast twitch muscle fibres are used. These are for the more explosive activities, which need quick reactions. They contract fast and produce a powerful action. They have only a limited oxygen supply and so tire quickly. Under a microscope they are white in colour. They are best used for speed events, throwing and jumping.

Slow twitch muscle fibres

The nervous system can detect when an event is slow and prolonged and will activate the slow twitch muscle fibres. These are more suited to endurance activities. They can contract many times and stay efficient over long periods. They have a very good oxygen supply, which gives them their energy. Under a microscope they are red in colour. They are suited to events that take a long time to complete, such as long distance running, cycling and swimming.

Explosive events like the discus, here performed by Shelley Drew, rely on fast twitch muscle fibres.

Slow twitch muscle fibres are needed in long-distance events.

What to do:

1. Read the paragraphs on the types of fibres in the muscles.
2. Make two columns headed FTMF and STMF.
3. List four main points for each type of fibre.

●●●● ▶ **Active Challenge**

In pairs, take turns in naming a sport. Your partner should say whether it needs fast or slow twitch muscle fibres for greatest success.

7 Muscle Tone and Posture

Muscle tone is voluntary muscles' readiness to work and be in a prepared state to react. Each muscle has slight tension, waiting to be used. A person's muscles never completely rest; the nearest they come to resting is when a person is asleep. Muscles' state of slight contraction helps with **posture**. The abdominals' toned state helps keep in place the internal organs of that area.

Posture relates to the way the body is supported by the muscles, whether standing, sitting or moving. In some activities where the look of the performer is important to the result, like gymnastics, diving and dance, good posture is vital, it increases the marks awarded to the performer and enhances the performance. When muscles are trained, their tone increases and this can help posture.

There are several advantages of having good posture:

- When breathing, there is more room for the lungs to expand and operate; round shoulders make it hard to breathe properly.
- The heart needs to be given enough space to function properly and beat without hindrance.
- The digestive system works well if it has the space to do its job properly.
- Bone alignment prevents strain and injury – poor posture can strain the bones, tendons and ligaments i.e. fallen arches.
- There is more energy available when the body is in alignment as the muscles do not have to work so hard to keep the body stable. (Like carrying a ladder, if it is vertical it is easy to carry, if it is at an angle more energy is required to carry it.)
- Maintaining good posture can help the shape of a person. In turn, self-esteem is increased if a person feels good about the way they look. A person standing or sitting well can give a good impression to others.

Good and bad posture

What to do:

Part A

1. Look carefully at the picture showing two different postures.
2. Describe what you see.
3. Think about the head, shoulder, stomach and hip positions.

Part B

1. Complete a spidergram relating to good posture using the words from the paragraph on Muscle Tone and Posture.

Key Terms:

Antagonist	► relaxing muscle allowing movement
Fast twitch muscle fibres	► muscle fibres used in events requiring quick reactions and power
Muscle tone	► muscles' state of slight tension and readiness to work
Posture	► the way the muscles hold the body when still or in motion
Prime mover	► contracting muscle causing movement
Slow twitch muscle fibres	► muscle fibres required in endurance events

Task 7

Muscle strength

Strength can be defined as a maximum weight lifted or moved in one try. By repeating strength exercises the size of the muscle increases. A person who would take advantage of an increase in muscle size would be a rugby player in the scrum or any activity where bulk is an advantage. The strength of tendons, ligaments and bone will increase too. Weight training is a method used to improve muscular strength. To do this an athlete would lift heavy weights for a few repetitions.

When the muscles increase in size, this is called **hypertrophy**. If training stops then muscles lose their size, the muscle is said to **atrophy**. When muscles are overworked, they cannot contract, fatigue sets in and the muscles cannot work any more. After intensive stress on a muscle, cramp can often result. This contraction or spasm of the muscle happens automatically due to a build-up of lactic acid in the muscle. Massage and gentle moving of the part help to relieve the pain.

A weight lifter, like Belarus' Gennady Oleschuk, seen here at Sydney Olympics 2000, concentrates on developing muscular strength in training.

Muscle endurance

Endurance is the ability to keep working over a long period without tiring. People who take part in events that take a long time to complete need muscular endurance. These events include long distance running, cycling and swimming. To improve muscular endurance an athlete will lift light weights many times.

When training for a specific activity the body should be prepared so that it can perform the skills needed throughout the event without losing effectiveness. The body remembers how to perform tasks properly due to a regular training pattern. Regular exercise improves fitness. Activities that increase the heart rate above 75% of its maximum, for 20 minutes, five times a week, will generally make a person fitter.

A person should be able to carry out daily tasks without getting out of breath. Each job requires a different level of fitness to complete the tasks involved successfully. An office worker will be fit to do their job, as a window cleaner will be fit to do theirs.

A top-class long-distance runner has sinewy muscles that can keep working over long periods.

Increasing the strength around a damaged area such as a joint is important to a **rehabilitating** player. This will give strength to the damaged area and make it less likely to be injured again. A rehabilitation programme, specific to the performer, will be designed according to their needs. Some serious injuries need rehabilitation over many months. Part of the programme would start with moving light weights many times. Gradually, the amount of stress on the injured area is increased; this is achieved by increasing the amount of weight to be moved.

Part of the job of training is to repeat actions needed in the game so that when they are called for, they can be applied to the game. This will train the muscles to repeat actions at the appropriate speed and position.

What to do:

1. What happens to muscles when they are trained for strength?

2. What happens to muscles when they are trained for endurance?

> Ideas to include are: size, strength, tone and type of exercise.

Key Terms:

Atrophy	▶ when muscle loses its size because of lack of exercise
Hypertrophy	▶ when muscle increases in size because of exercise
Muscular endurance	▶ muscles' ability to keep working over long periods of time without tiring
Muscular strength	▶ muscles' ability to lift or move a maximum weight in one attempt
Rehabilitate	▶ recovery from injury

Summary

The body uses three types of muscle. Some can be controlled consciously; others work automatically. The greatest amount of muscle is voluntary muscle, which makes up about 40% of the body. Tendons attach the bone to muscle. Tendons can be different in shape. For instance, the scapula is a flat (plate) bone, therefore the tendon attaching the triceps are broad and flat too.

For movement to take place, the muscles work as antagonistic pairs. There are many pairs of muscles in the body but the ones to concentrate on are the biceps and triceps, and the quadriceps and hamstrings. There are two different ways muscles contract. When sudden bursts of energy are needed, fast twitch muscle fibres are used. When moderate effort over a long period is required, then slow twitch muscle fibres come into operation. When you are awake your muscles are in a constant state of readiness to work: this is called muscle tone. This tone helps to maintain good posture. Holding your body, whilst standing, in as straight a line as possible helps internal systems work without hindrance.

Training can make muscles stronger. Training and practice help the body to remember how to complete tasks well. After training for strength, the muscles will hypertrophy. Strength coupled with speed will give the power required to complete explosive events when the fast twitch muscle fibres are used.

Exercising for endurance will help an athlete perform long distance events. This kind of exercise requires moderate effort and takes a long time to complete. Slow twitch muscle fibres arc used in long distance events.

Analysis of Performance

What you will learn about in this section:

1. The Importance of Rules and their Application
2. Observation and Analysis of Performance
3. Evaluate by Comparing With the Perfect Model
4. Planning to Improve Performance
5. Leadership and Your Sport

The *Analysis of Performance* part of the course requires candidates to recognise the strengths and weaknesses of a performance and to understand and demonstrate ways to improve it. To do this you will experience a variety of roles and responsibilities linked with physical activity. As your personal performance continually develops, so should your abilities in the five areas making up the analysis and performance section.

Importance of rules and their application in sport

Evaluate a performance by comparing it with the perfect model

Planning to improve performance

Observation and analysis of performance

Leadership and your sport

ANALYSIS OF PERFORMANCE

This section of work will develop your skills as an official, coach and leader in your chosen sport. It will link the application of skills with factors affecting participation and performance parts of the specification. Your overall success in this part of the course relies on reaching a good standard in each component. A weak area will affect your overall analysis of performance mark.

The following coaching model is useful when breaking down the parts that are important for analysis.

Performance	**Observation**	**Analysis**
Actions of player/participant.	Action watched carefully by another.	Parts of the performance studied in detail.

Feedback	**Planning**	**Evaluation**
Information given to the performer responding to the results of competition and training.	Consideration of what training will be best for future improvement based on the strengths and weaknesses of the performance.	Performance compared with the 'perfect model' and past performances.

1 The Importance of Rules and their Application

It is important that you gain as much information as you can about the rules from your chosen sport. Ways to increase your knowledge and understanding:

- watch sports events on TV and listen to the commentary of the experts
- play your chosen sport to as high a standard as you can
- read coaching manuals and the rules of your sport
- discuss rules with your teacher
- practice refereeing or umpiring
- use the Internet to find information on rules.

 **Active Challenge**

For your chosen sport find five books you can use to help with your knowledge of the rules. You could use the Internet to help find the titles of these publications.

2 Observation and Analysis of Performance

Many people can watch a sporting activity, but only the trained eye can see what the performer is really attempting to do. The observation and analysis part of the course requires you to develop these skills and make a judgement on quality, success and ways of improving a performance.

Skills needed

The skills you will develop are similar to those needed by coaches in order to get the best out of their players.

Applying rules – show knowledge and application of them, practice and experience in this area can be gained from officiating in or judging a sport.

Using specialised terminology – each sport has its own language for describing skills, tactics and strategies. Using this language shows an understanding of the sport.

Analysing – be able to break down the action of the performer.

Recording – a record of the performance gives information, which can be analysed and acted upon; a training session may be changed according to the results.

Evaluating – watching a performer in action and working out how close their performance is to what is known as the 'perfect model'.

Identifying the perfect model – analysing the performance, knowledge and understanding of what the best performance looks like are very important. Any performance can then be compared to this 'perfect model'.

Seeing strengths and weaknesses – each performance has positive and negative aspects and both must be recognised by the observer.

Communicating – being able to communicate a breakdown of the action to the performer so improvements can be made. Even in weak performances it is important to comment on a good aspect in order to keep the performer motivated.

Planning – by working out the successes and failures of the performance, planned changes can be made to improve training, tactics and strategies.

Applying knowledge – of training methods/principles is essential when linking with weaknesses and strengths of the performer. The principles and methods will determine what goes in the training programme.

Understanding leadership – good leadership is the ability to get the best out of the performer. Give examples of successful captains/coaches/managers. Leading through example, motivating, setting up achievable targets and rewarding progress.

What to do:

1. For each of the 11 skill areas, make a list of the experiences you have already.
2. Re-list the skills with the areas you most need to work on at the top, moving down to the ones you are most confident in at the bottom.

Observation

Observation needs to be planned. In order to observe a performance meaningfully, an understanding of the perfect model is necessary. Where you observe the action from is important: standing at different positions in relation to the action will give different views and more than one viewpoint may be necessary for a full picture of an activity.

Equipment

Whatever method of analysis you use it will be useful to have a record of the performance. This will act as evidence and can then be used with other data to analyse the results of the performance at a later date. Plan your observations well. Record sheets, pencils and something to lean on are all basic and obvious requirements to do the job. Prepare the equipment you need in advance so that you can concentrate on the process of observation. You may prefer to photograph or video the performance. In that case, greater planning is necessary to book the equipment in advance.

The view

Where to watch from may vary according to the sport. A team game has lots of action so being near to the performers' positional area is good. A raised viewpoint is often useful. For smaller playing areas like volleyball, badminton and tennis, court side is effective and, if possible, a raised position may give a better view.

The spidergram suggests places to stand when watching a team game.

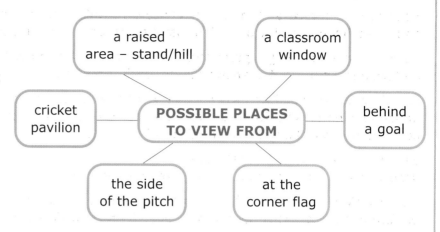

What to do:

1. For three sports, decide on the best viewing position for each. You can use diagrams in your answer if you wish.
2. Say why you think some sports are best viewed at different positions, such as judo viewed at ground level, but team games from a high position.

Gaining observational experience

There are different ways in which you can build up your observational skills. Using as many methods as you can will give you the broadest information base from which to work.

By watching an activity and then discussing the performance with others, you develop your knowledge, language and understanding of what you see.

Listen to the coaching points given by a teacher and then compare them with how a person performs the activity. This gives experience of linking the description of the correct action with a beginner's attempt.

Reading coaching manuals and books will give you knowledge of what the perfect model should look like. These books break down the skill and illustrate or describe the parts of the action to concentrate on. This knowledge of the components of the correct skill can be watched for and compared with that of the observed performance. You can than decide on the strengths and weaknesses of the action you see.

Once you understand the skill you will appreciate how it can be broken down. For instance in gymnastics, a judge will look for the following when marking a vault: flight on, flight off, elevation, shape of the body, distance carried, body alignment and controlled landing. It is these areas that the observer must be aware of in order to understand the action. As the vault only takes a short time to complete, videoing the action will help you concentrate on one part of the action at a time. You can then build up your observation and appreciation of the whole action after several replays.

Knowing a game well allows the observer to anticipate the action, prepare a mental picture of the best performance and compare it with what they see. This expectation of the action also allows the effectiveness of the build-up play to be observed too.

Ways to observe

There are various ways of watching top-class performers, each with positive and negative points for the observer. Some of these methods are readily available through watching television and reading newspapers and magazines, whereas some need seeking out through libraries and the Internet.

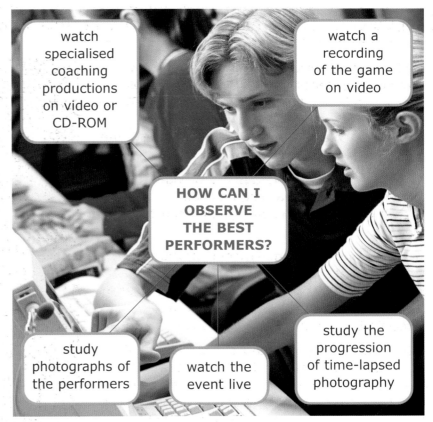

watch specialised coaching productions on video or CD-ROM

watch a recording of the game on video

HOW CAN I OBSERVE THE BEST PERFORMERS?

study photographs of the performers

watch the event live

study the progression of time-lapsed photography

Knowledge of skill-related fitness

What you have learnt about skill-related fitness and its application to different sports will help with your observations. You will know which components to look out for in your chosen activity.

Co-ordination – the ability to use two parts of the body at the same time.

Agility – the ability to change direction quickly and maintain control of the whole body.

Speed – the fastest rate at which a person can complete a task or cover a distance.

SKILL-RELATED FITNESS COMPONENTS

Reaction time – the time it takes to respond to a stimulus.

Power – the ability to apply a combination of strength and speed in an action.

Balance – the ability to keep the body stable whether still, moving or in a different shape by keeping the centre of gravity over the base.

●●●● ▶ **Active Challenge**

Using a sport of your choice, state a basic, an intermediate and an advanced skill.

3 Evaluate by Comparing With the Perfect Model

In order to realise whether a sporting action is good or not an understanding of how the action should look in its perfect state should be appreciated. This is the 'perfect model' you will mark any performance against. There are several ways you can observe the perfect model:

- world-class sports coverage (TV or video)
- training videos or coaching manuals
- action photos from magazines and books of top players

When developing an understanding of the perfect model it is useful to use video recordings of the best performers. This allows replays and pauses in the action to be made, giving time for you to appreciate the performance in question.

When looking at a performance, the shape of the body in action will indicate how close it is to the perfect model. Some areas to look for are the head position, where the centre of gravity is, a balanced body position and how the weight is distributed.

What to do:

1. Look at the two photos above and compare the differences in the following:
   - head position
   - balance of the body
   - centre of gravity
   - weight distribution.

Task 3

Expectations of the observer

Many factors can influence the way a skill is performed. These are sometimes in the control of the performer and sometimes not. The observer should distinguish between the two and adapt the comments given in feedback accordingly. For instance, a player may well have shown success in a skill in the past, but changes in the weather may cause the skill to break down.

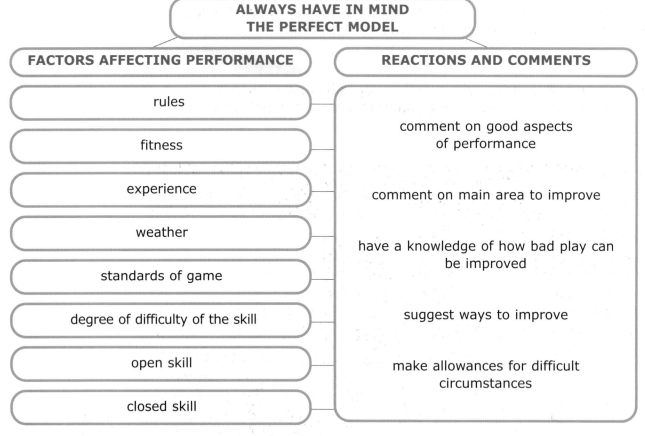

Factors influencing the expectation and reaction of the observer

How to gain experience of what to say

Saying the right things is important. Too many negative comments and the performer will lose confidence and the skill will remain poor; too much praise and they may stop trying or become complacent.

There are several ways to gain experience of what to say to a performer. Listening to and watching different types of TV sports programmes, radio commentary, coaching points given by a teacher and interviews with sportspeople and their coaches will help you to build up the correct language. Each method has its own style and content – a certain style may suit you better than others. Language used will include technical terms, comments on skill, opinions on performance and factual analysis.

Educational, instructive and coaching videos will put technical language in context giving you a greater understanding of the activity.

 **Active Challenge**

Think about what technical terms you know for your chosen sport and how these will help you when giving feedback.

How to communicate what you see

It is important to make comments to the performer as clear, positive and to the point as possible.

- Pick out the skills to comment on.
- Look for good points – speed, aim, body position, movement, direction of performer.
- Start with praise – how the performer was successful.
- Identify the most ineffective part of the skill and say how it can be improved.
- Suggest how this skill can be worked on – for example, improvement of leg strength, more vigorous arm action and better co-ordination.

What to do:

1. Decide on a skill to analyse or refer to the photograph of Kath Johnson below. Use the indicated points to make comments about the performer.

head position
(eyes watching ball)

alignment of
the body

centre of gravity
(low and over base)

grip on the stick

balanced and
stable base

feet position

Factors building up to the perfect model

Ways to analyse

Comments made on a performance can be based on subjective or objective evidence: each can comment about the same action but in a different way.

Subjective

Subjective analysis is related to how the observer thinks the player is performing in comparison with the other players. Two people may have different opinions about a particular performance. The list below includes subjective statements:

'That's the best goal I've seen him score.' 'She looks to be serving better.'

'She is moving more quickly to the ball.' 'I thought that shot had more pace.'

'There seem to be fewer double faults than in previous sets.' 'She is crossing the ball better.'

Objective

Objective analysis is based on fact, not personal opinions. The aim is to have results and statistics to support the observations. This type of analysis is helpful to the coach and performer as it identifies explicitly the strengths and weaknesses of the performer. Objective analysis provides:

- statistical record of aspects of the performance
- records of heights jumped, distances thrown and speeds run
- comparisons made between performer and the decided criteria (perfect model).

What to do:

1. For a sport of your choice:

   a Give three examples of subjective comments.

   b State why objective comments are more accurate.

   c Give examples of how an individual can be seen to be successful in the sport.

Analysis

There are a variety of areas that can be analysed when looking at performance. Some are more complex than others. The most straightforward range from individual, closed and basic skills to the complexities of the open complex, advanced skills.

There are different skills required by different players on the pitch and the observer must be mindful of this in the analysis. An attacker may not need information on the number of tackles they make, but for a defender, this would be an important part of the analysis. A strong team may be often on the attack, so their defence is only rarely involved. As a result, a defender may only make a few passes in the game, so for them, the percentage rather than the actual number of successful passes made may reveal more about personal play.

The skills required for good play are different for a defender and attacker.

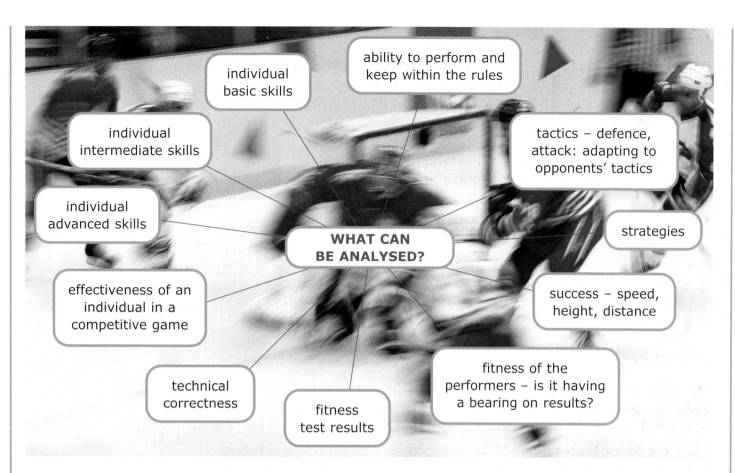

Mind map with centre node **WHAT CAN BE ANALYSED?** connected to:
- individual basic skills
- ability to perform and keep within the rules
- individual intermediate skills
- tactics – defence, attack: adapting to opponents' tactics
- individual advanced skills
- strategies
- effectiveness of an individual in a competitive game
- success – speed, height, distance
- technical correctness
- fitness of the performers – is it having a bearing on results?
- fitness test results

Different ways to record and analyse

Keeping a record of a person's performance can be done in several ways. Records taken at different times in the season are useful as they can show individual progress, the effectiveness of training and strengths and weaknesses of performance.

The methods used to record performance vary and can include:

- Detailed notes made by the observer based on the action of the performer.
- Check list for performance – this lists what the person needs to perform to complete the action and represents the perfect model. The observed performance can be compared to the components on the list and a simple 'tick-off' system can be used.
- Individual's performance in the game – this records the actions of an individual in the game situation. The success or failure of the performer is recorded each time they are an active part of the game and can be indicated by a plus or minus response to stated criteria. In tennis, for example, there are many parts to the game important to record; such as the number of points won on first or second serve, or number of double-faults recorded.
- team performance – this records the effectiveness of the team performance. It reflects the success of the chosen tactics and can include:
  - where successful shots come from
  - where on the pitch/court the attacks start
  - where the opposition attacks come from
  - how many corners the team earn.

 **Active Challenge**

With a partner, choose a basic skill you are confident in performing. Break down the skill, listing in order the different actions needed to complete the action.

What to do:

1. For a sport of your choice:

   a make a list of the parts of the game that can be recorded to give useful feedback to the coach

   b make a record sheet of your list that could be used when observing the game.

Evaluating

Evaluating a performance by comparing it with the perfect model is the process after analysis when the observer works out the success or failure of an activity. Evaluation tells us where strengths and weaknesses lie and how training should be adapted in the light of the findings in order to make progress.

Knowledge of the perfect model may come from a photograph, video or coaching manual. Understanding the perfect model will make it easier to evaluate what is seen and to suggest improvements to be made.

The evaluation process may look like this:

1 Perfect model – know what you are looking for.

2 Make observations of the performance.

3 Compare the performance with the perfect model.

4 Decide on and state the main positive point to express.

5 Decide on and state the main fault and express it.

6 Communicate how the performance can be improved at the next attempt (short term).

7 Communicate how training will need to be adapted and a new plan made (long term).

Feedback

To work on and develop skill, every performer needs feedback. An athlete may have technical feedback after their event, but a team may need a combination of skill and tactical feedback. Whatever the content of the feedback if it is not acted upon then it is of no use. The observer may include comments on motivation, tactics, commitment, skill, determination and effort.

There are factors that you should be aware of when giving feedback and they should influence what you say and how you say it. For instance, if someone has only just started participating in the activity there may be many mistakes and negative comments would be inappropriate. Detailed comments on their faults could well demoralise the performer.

It is the coach or manager's role to supply feedback to the performers. They choose the most appropriate way to deliver the information, which may be given individually, to the whole team, or to groups within the team – such as the defence and attack.

Feedback can benefit performers by keeping them motivated, working towards achievable goals, allowing them to see development in fitness and in fitness tests results. The coach can plan the training programme around the feedback, use it as a motivating tool and change tactics to hide weaknesses and show strengths.

What to do:

1. This work involves practice in analysing results and feeding back information. Study the analysis sheet of a game of tennis. Interpret the results by including comments on:

   where the most successful play is coming from

   where the least successful play is coming from

   how the tactics should change

   the training that should be included in the programme as a result.

Tennis analysis sheet

Tennis	Set 1	Set 2	Set 3
aces	1	3	2
1st serve percentage	52%	70%	72%
2nd serve percentage	60%	74%	70%
speed of serve	120mph	122mph	123mph
double faults	2	1	0
forehand winners	8	6	7
backhand winners	5	7	5
volley winners	11	18	19
un-forced errors	8	6	6

4 Planning to Improve Performance

Having fully analysed the performer's action and identified where their strengths and weaknesses are located, you need to draw up a training plan. This plan will help to organise the training necessary to correct the faults and maintain the strengths, bringing an effective balance to the practice sessions. It will also enable the performer to peak for a particular event. For instance, you would not wish your performer to be training intensively right up to the time that are due to compete – it is important that your performer arrives fresh and full of energy.

How to read the results

Reading and interpreting results is essential to planning. A coach (or analyst) may look at an individual performance, compare two players, the team performance or how two teams' statistics compared.

- Count the actions to identify strengths.
- Count the actions to identify weaknesses.
- Compare success and failure of each action.
- Compare with past performance records.
- Compare two players'/teams' performances.

Considerations for the coach

The coach will also take into consideration questions such as:

- When did the faults occur – if late in the game is fitness the problem?
- In what situation was the error – did the fault(s) happen in pressured situations?
- Is the fault in skill – will identifying the component of skill-related fitness and then training that area help?
- Is the skill new – was the player playing out of position?
- What were the opposition like – was it the hardest match of the season?
- Was the error tactical – would working on using judgement and understanding of the tactics improve performance?
- Has the performer reached a plateau of improvement? (Seemingly no progress is made for a time, skills must be broken down and worked on separately, this is frustrating for the performer and coach – patience will have to be shown to give time to go beyond this.)

Decisions to be made

After deciding on which areas need improvement, the practices and training plans are adapted. The coach may show the performer examples of the perfect model or the new targets to work towards, so a clear picture of what is necessary is identified.

Changes

- New training programme put in place with increased emphasis on weak areas.
- Make sure that skill practices are relevant and help the performer to improve.
- In practice sessions, performer should perform the skill slowly and then build up the pace.
- Set new achievable targets – number of repetitions, weights to lift.
- Use static opponents to build up skill and confidence in the performer and gradually progress to realistic opposition.
- Fitness training with an emphasis on aerobic work will provide stamina so a player can maintain a performance throughout a match.

A coach needs to take note of a player's performance, identify areas that need to improve and put them into the training programme. A good coach will discuss reasons for changes to training sessions with the performer based on past results.

What to do:

1. Using your chosen sport as the example, write three sentences on each of the following as though you are a coach:
   - stamina
   - strength
   - co-ordination
   - speed
   - passive/aggressive opposition
   - tactical awareness
   - identifying the perfect model.

> **Example:** "You narrowly missed out and came second in your last race. More work on a quicker sprint finish will give you a better chance. We will start by doing speed work at the end of the next training session." (Speed)

5 Leadership and Your Sport

People who can motivate and get the best performance out of others, even in difficult circumstances, have leadership qualities. There are many personalities in sport who are successful leaders. Managers, coaches and captains all play their part in motivating their team. As football is so widely televised many of its leaders are well known.

How leadership enhances performance

- Style of leadership influences the performer.
- Leader sets achievable goals.
- Leader keeps players informed about their progress.
- Leader is respected for their knowledge/experience and history in the sport.

Role of the captain

- To influence their team and individual players both on and off the pitch.
- Lead by example as a role model.
- Talk to players throughout a game to encourage, praise, change play and so on.
- Encourage or lead others through their fear.
- Give instructions on tactics.
- Keep the team playing together and working hard.
- Act as a link between the players and the officials.

Role of the coach

- Take training sessions.
- Identify and recognise strengths and weaknesses.
- Give individual help to performers.
- Treat performers as individuals as far as possible.
- Know the players and set achievable goals that suit their personality.
- Reward good work.
- Organise players' diets.
- Motivate training sessions.
- Make training interesting and fun.

Role of the manager

- Organise team.
- Put the right blend of characters together – they may not be the most skilful but they work hard for each other.
- Support and discipline players.
- Praise and criticise play.
- Represent the team in the media.

 **Active Challenge**

Choose a coach, captain or manager who has really impressed you. Prepare a short account to present to the rest of the class of why they have done so. (Use an example other than football if you can.)

To gain experience of what it is like to be a coach, take a session based on your performer fitness testing and analysis of performance. This is a good way to put into operation your understanding of the work. It may not be right first time, so listen to advice from the teacher and improve on your next effort.

Simple guide to refereeing

It looks simple to referee, but it is a skill needing practice and understanding. A good referee will not make a game better, but can prevent one being spoilt. A referee needs to keep up with the action, watch carefully and make quick, correct decisions on play.

Equipment – suitable clothing, whistle, pencil, score sheet and relevant disciplinary card if appropriate.

Knowledge of rules – know the rules and be able to apply them quickly.

Position – each game has a preferred position in relation to the action, adopt the appropriate one, keep up with play so you have a close view of the action, know the position for special plays – corners, free throws and so on.

Hand signals – know and use the recognised hand signals for the game, these help make your decision clear to those players away from the action.

Order of reaction – see the offence, blow the whistle, state the offence, give the correct signal/announce your decision, let play commence on your decision.

Words to use – use the recognised terminology for the offence, (for example, in netball there are two types of offence – one leading to a free pass the other to a penalty pass, this should be clearly stated).

Mark allocation

How much is all this worth? For each of the five sections, four marks are available which go towards your final overall mark:

1 Rules and their application in sport

2 Observation and analysis

3 Evaluate by comparing with the perfect model

4 Planning to improve performance

5 Leadership and your sport.

It is therefore important to work hard in each of the areas and so increase your chances of a good grade. If you can show understanding and practical application it can add 10% to your overall mark.

Your chosen sport

Throughout the course you will be asked to assess your own and others' performances. Gain as much experience as you can by analysing performance in practical sports lessons. For the examination, you will have to name the sport you are analysing, so make yourself as familiar with that sport as possible. Factors affecting your choice may include:

- it is your favourite sport or your best performance sport
- it is the sport you know most about
- it is a sport with lots of readily available information available
- it is a sport with simple tactics and basic skills, easy to understand and analyse.

Preparation

Use this list to check that you have done as much as you can to earn the best mark:

- know your sport
- know the perfect model
- be able to use the correct terminology
- know tactics – basic, intermediate, advanced
- have gained experience watching and reading about your chosen sport
- have joined in class discussions to increase your confidence in verbally expressing your thoughts
- have umpired/refereed or judged your sport so you are confident with the rules, regulations and procedures
- have completed, recorded and saved for reference, several examples of your analyses
- have records of past analysis to hand to revise from
- have practised recording performance so it can be done quickly allowing you to concentrate on the action.

On the day of your analysis

- If possible, organise your favoured position for observing the action.
- Have all the equipment you need to record the action.
- Have in mind the perfect model performance.
- Be confident that you have revised well enough to succeed.

You will be asked questions about a performance in your chosen sport. What to do:

- listen to the instructions
- listen to the questions
- think your answer through in your head before you speak
- keep calm and give a full, informative, clear answer which is as brief as necessary without being vague
- if appropriate, give examples from your knowledge of the perfect model.

You are bound to be a little nervous but you can draw confidence from the fact that, if you have completed all the necessary preparations, tasks and analysis as coursework, you are being examined from a position of strength.

Glossary

A

Abduction   moving a limb or bone away from the body

Adduction   moving a limb or bone towards the body

Aerobic   'with oxygen'; when exercise is moderate and steady, the heart can supply all the oxygen the working muscles need

Aesthetic quality   how good an action looks

Agility   the ability to change the position of the body quickly and to control the movement of the whole body easily

Alveoli   tiny air sacs of the lungs where gaseous exchange takes place

Anaerobic   'without oxygen'; when exercising in short, fast bursts, the heart cannot supply blood and oxygen to the muscles as fast as the cells can use them, so energy is released without oxygen present

Antagonist   a muscle whose action counteracts that of another muscle and so allowing movement

Aorta   the main artery of the body, blood vessel transporting oxygenated blood to the body tissues

Arterioles   blood vessels that are sub-divisions of arteries, leading into capillaries

Asymmetric bars   a piece of Olympic gymnastic equipment used by females with bars at different heights

Atrophy   decline in effectiveness, when muscles atrophy they weaken and lose their strength and size

B

Balance   the ability to retain the centre of mass (gravity) of the body above the base of support with reference to static (stationary) or dynamic (changing) conditions of movement, shape and orientation

Balanced competition   grouping based on size, age or experience for an even match

Balanced diet   daily intake of food containing right amounts and types of nutrients

Basal metabolic rate   the level at which energy is used without exercise

Blood doping   method of increasing the oxygen carrying capacity of the blood, by increasing haemoglobin levels and red blood cell count

Body composition   the proportion of body weight that is fat, muscle and bone, normally measured as a percentage

C

Calcify   harden by conversion into calcium carbonate

Calcium   an essential element for strong healthy bones, dairy products provide a good source of calcium

Cancelluos bone   name for spongy bone; has air pockets so it looks like a sponge

Capillaries   blood vessels of hair-like thinness that connect the arteries with the veins

Carbohydrate loading   eating large amounts of carbohydrate-rich foods to build up glycogen levels in the body to use in endurance events

Cardiac muscle   only found in the heart, never tires

Cardiac output   the amount of blood pumped by the heart in one minute

Cardiovascular   relating to the heart and blood vessels

Cardiovascular fitness   the ability to exercise the entire body for long periods of time, this is dependent on the fitness of the heart, blood and blood vessels

Cartilage   whitish, tough, flexible tissue found at the end of bones, more widespread in infants, as during growth it is replaced by bone

Cervical vertebrae   bones of the vertebrae forming the neck

Circuit training   a series of exercises completed in order and for a certain time limit

Circulatory system   transports blood, using the heart, through all parts of the body

Classification   a way of sorting or organising groups

Coccyx   small fused triangular bone at the base of the vertebral column

Compact bone   strong, hard bone

Compound/open fracture   break of the bone that pierces the skin, causing a risk of infection

Concussion   injury to the brain, caused by blow to the head, may cause a person temporarily to lose consciousness

Continuous training   aerobic exercising, at a moderate to high level, with no rests lasting for a sustained period of time

Convalescence   period of time when body is rested to aid recovery

Cool down   exercises after the main activity gradually bringing the body systems back to near resting state

Co-ordination   the ability to perform complex moves using two or more body parts together

Cross training   using different training methods in the same session

D

Dehydration   extreme lack of water in the body, usually as a result of exercising in hot conditions or heavy sweating

Diaphragm   a dome-shaped muscle that divides the chest cavity from the abdominal cavity

Diaphysis   shaft or central part of a long bone

Dilate   open up or become wider

Dislocate   disturb the usual arrangement of bones so that they move out of their usual joint arrangement

DRABC   **D**anger (to casualty or first aider?) **R**esponse (different levels of casualty response – alert/unresponsive; presence or absence of voice/pain?) **A**irway (is there a blockage of the airway?) **B**reathing (is casualty breathing?) **C**irculation (is the blood circulating?)

Drugs   substances (other than food) that, when taken into the body, cause a change; socially unacceptable drugs are drugs that are illegal to possess

E

Ectomorph   body type with little fat or muscle and a narrow shape

Element   a part that contributes to the whole

Emergency procedures   series of actions to be followed in a crisis

Endomorph   body type that is apple or pear shaped, with a large amount of fat

Endothelium   internal space of the blood vessels

Endurance   the ability to keep working over a period of time without tiring or losing skill

Energy drinks   fluids containing carbohydrates

Epiphysis   end of a long bone

Etiquette   a code of polite behaviour

Exercise   a form of physical activity done primarily to improve one's health and physical fitness

Expiration   breathing out, exhalation

Extension   increasing the angle at a joint

F

Fartlek training   'speed play', changing speed, distances and times of exercise, with rests in the same session

Fast twitch muscle fibres used in events requiring quick reactions and power, muscles contract rapidly providing strength and so tire quickly

Fatigue extreme tiredness and physical exhaustion

Fibrinogen a protein found in blood plasma that helps clotting

Fitness ability to meet the demands of the environment

FITT frequency, intensity, time and type

Flat bone also called plate bone, mainly linked with protection

Flexibility joint's ability to move to their full range

Flexion decreasing the angle at a joint

Forced breathing breathing during exercise

Friction action of two surfaces rubbing together creating heat

Fused two or more bones knitted together so no movement occurs

G

Glycogen the form in which carbohydrates are stored in the muscle and liver

Governing body a group responsible for rules, procedures and fixtures of a particular game or event

H

Haemoglobin found in red blood cells, transports oxygen to body tissue

Health a state of complete social, mental and physical well-being

Heart rate the number of times the heart beats per minute

Heat exhaustion fatigue brought on by the body temperature rising

Hypertrophy when muscle increases in size due to regular exercise

Hypothermia condition of the body when its core temperature falls below 35°C

I

Individual needs personal requirements for training

Inflamed reddened and swollen

Infringement action in a game that breaks the rules

Insertion the point where a tendon attaches a muscle to bone where there is movement

Inspiration the drawing in of breath, inhalation

Interval training mixing periods of hard exercise with rest periods

Involuntary muscles muscles that work automatically, controlled by the involuntary nervous system

Irregular bones bones that have no uniform shape

Isometric muscular contraction muscle contraction with no movement, there is increased tension but the length of the muscles does not alter, e.g. when pressing against a stationary object

Isotonic muscular contraction muscle contraction that results in limb movement

J

Joint the point where two or more bones meet

L

Lactic acid produced in the muscle tissues during strenuous exercise, as a result of insufficient oxygen availability

Leverage   the use of force or effort (muscle power) to overcome resistance

Ligament   tough, rounded, elastic fibre attaching bone to bone

Long bones   those bones that are the longest in the body which make up the arms and legs

Lumbar vertebrae   bones of the vertebrae in the lower back region

M

Main activity   period of training, competition or performance when all-out effort is applied

Masking agent   a legal substance for a sport, hiding the presence of an illegal one

Maximum heart rate   calculated as 220 minus age

Mesomorph   body that is characterised by being muscular

Metabolic rate   the speed at which energy is used up

Minimum level of fitness (for health)   the resulting fitness level when over a period of weeks three to five exercise sessions of 20 minutes, raising the heart rate to 60–80% of its maximum are completed

Moderation   balancing training and not over-training

Modified game   a game with adapted rules, equipment and playing area based on a full game

Movement   in motion, could be an action like running or swinging a racket at a ball

Muscle definition   muscle shape

Muscle tone   muscles in a state of very slight tension, ready and waiting to be used

Muscular endurance   the ability to use voluntary muscles, over long periods of time without getting tired

Muscular strength   the amount of force a muscle can exert against a resistance in one attempt

N

Nausea   feeling of sickness

Newton   a unit of force

O

Obese   a term used to describe people who are very overfat

Optimum weight   ideal weight for a person, giving them the best chance of success in an activity

Origin   the point where the tendon attaches the muscle to a fixed bone

Ossification   the development from cartilage to bone

Osteoblasts   bone-forming cells

Osteoclasts   bone-eroding cells

Overfat   a person having more body fat than is recommended for their gender and height

Overload   following the principle that the body can only be improved through training more and harder than normal

Overuse injury   this can be caused by using a part of the body too much or by too much repetitive training

Overweight   having weight in excess of normal, not harmful unless accompanied by overfatness

Oxygen debt   the amount of oxygen consumed during recovery above that which would have been consumed in the same time at rest (this results in a shortfall in the oxygen available)

P

Performance   how well a task is completed

Performance-enhancing drugs   substances that artificially improve personal characteristics and performance

Periosteal collar   also known as periosteum, membrane surrounding the shaft of a bone

Personal exercise programme (PEP) training designed specifically for one individual

Posture the way the muscles hold the body when still or in motion

Power the ability to complete strength performances quickly; power = strength x speed

Prime mover contracting muscles that cause movement

Principles of training ideas behind effects of training

Progression starting slowly and gradually increasing the amount of exercise completed

Protect guard against threat

Pulmonary circuit system of blood vessels that transports deoxygenated blood from the heart to the lungs and re-oxygenated blood back again

R

Reaction time the time between the presentation of a stimulus and the onset of a movement

Recovery rate the time it takes for the heart and metabolism to return to resting after exercise

Regularity repeating exercise sessions in a week to bring about improved fitness

Rehabilitate recovery from injury

Residual volume the amount of air left in the lungs after a maximal breath out

Resting heart rate number of heart beats per minute when the body is at rest

Reversibility any adaptation that takes place as a consequence of training will be reversed when a person stops training

RICE rest, ice, compression, elevation; order of treatment for a minor injury

Rotation movement in a circular or part-circular fashion

S

Sacrum bones of the vertebrae, fused in adults, making part of the pelvic girdle

Septum wall of muscle dividing the right and left sides of the heart, septum can also mean a dividing wall between two cavities elsewhere in the body

Shaft long, thin part of a long bone

Shape form or outline

Short bone smaller bone found in the hands and feet

Simple/closed fracture break of the bone when the skin is not broken

Skeleton the arrangement of the 206 bones of the human body

Skill-related fitness physical motor abilities of the body adapted to specific sports

Skin-fold calliper equipment used to measure a fold of skin with its underlying layer of fat

Slow twitch muscle fibres muscle fibres required in endurance events

Somatotype particular body type and shape of an individual, there are three types: ectomorph, endomorph and mesomorph

Specificity concentrating on specific kinds of activity or exercise to build specific body parts

Speed the differential rate at which an individual is able to perform a movement or cover a distance in a period of time

Stress a state of mental or emotional strain leading to anxiety and nervous tension

Stress-related illnesses illness such as heart attack, ulcer, high blood pressure

Stroke volume the amount of blood pumped out of the heart by each ventricle during one contraction

Synovial capsule tough fibre surrounding the synovial joint

Synovial fluid fluid helping to lubricate a synovial joint

Synovial joints freely moveable joints with ends covered in cartilage

Synovial membrane lining inside joint capsule where synovial fluid is produced

Systematic training planning a programme for an individual as a result of the effect of previous training

Systemic circuit part of the circulatory system concerned with transporting oxygenated blood from the heart to the body and de-oxygenated blood back to the heart again

T

Target zone level of effort applied, often keeping within aerobic levels but depending on specified training intensity

Tendon strong, non-elastic tissue attaching bone to muscle

Thoracic vertebrae bones of the vertebrae in the chest area

Throwing cage a secured enclosure around a throwing area

Tidal volume amount of air breathed in or out at rest

Training a planned programme which uses scientific principles to improve performance, skill, game ability and motor and physical fitness

U

Unconsciousness state of unawareness, an unwakening sleep

V

Valves openings allowing blood flow in one direction, found in the heart and veins

Vena cava blood vessel transporting deoxygenated blood back to the heart

Vertebral column irregular bones (vertebrae) that run the length of the body from head to rear, the column protects the spinal chord

Vital capacity the maximum amount of air that can be forcibly exhaled after breathing in as much as possible

VO$_2$ max maximum amount of oxygen the body can take in

Voluntary muscles skeletal muscles, attached to the skeleton, work consciously by the brain

W

Warm-up exercises gradually putting stresses on the body systems in preparation for the main activity

Weight training progressively lifting heavier weights to improve strength or lifting weights more often to improve stamina

Y

Yellow bone marrow substance found in the shaft of a long bone

Index

A

aerobic exercise 81, 108–9

aesthetic qualities 9

air 104–6

anaerobic fitness 109

analysis, performance 140–55

aorta (heart) 96–7

athletics 77

atrophy 24, 138

B

ball and socket joints 125, 128

basal metabolic rate (BMR) 48

bleep tests 26–7

blood 65, 99–100, 115, 117

BMI see body mass index

BMR see basal metabolic rate

body 16–17, 55–9

body mass index (BMI) 25, 54

bones 57, 112–23, 124

breathing 105–11

C

calcification 116–17

cancellous bone 118

cardiac output 100, 102

cardio-pulmonary resuscitation (CPR) 92

cartilage 88, 115–17, 125–7

circuit training 32–3

circulatory system 15, 96–103, 107

club membership 10–11

coaching 69, 152–3

comments 146–7, 150

compact bone 118

competition 10, 68

concussion 93

continuous training 42–3

contractions 30–1

cool down 82

CPR see cardio-pulmonary resuscitation

cross training 44–5

D

dance 77

dehydration 69, 94

diaphragm 105

diaphysis 116–17

diet 46–7, 49–52

dislocations 88, 127

dress 70–2

drugs 60–7

E

eating disorders 52, 54

endurance 15, 21, 28–9, 103, 138

energy 48–9, 110

epiphyses 116–18

equipment 71, 76, 78–9

etiquette 72

exercise 6–10, 12–17, 25–9, 81–3

exhaustion 101

expiration 106

F

fartlek training 40–1

fast twitch muscle fibres 136

fat 17, 54, 57

feedback 151

fibrinogens 100

fitness 12–19, 25

FITT *see* frequency, intensity, time and type

flat bones 119–20, 122

flexibility 16, 29, 82, 130

food types 46–7

football 74

fractures 88–89

frame sizes 17

free weights 36

frequency, intensity, time and type (FITT) 21–5, 41

fused bones 124

G

games 76

gymnastics 76

H

haemoglobin 99

health 7, 12–19, 46–67

heart 96–7, 101–3

heat exhaustion 101

height to weight chart 53

hinge joints 125, 128

hygiene 67

hypertrophy 138

hypothermia 93

I

individual exercise needs 13, 20

injuries 68–83, 84–95

inspiration 106

intensive exercises 82

interval training 38–40

irregular bones 119–22

isometric contractions 31

isotonic contractions 30

J

jewellery 72

joints 124–31

L

lactic acid 109

leadership 80, 153

ligaments 126–7

long bones 114–20, 122

lungs 105–6

M

machine weights 35

marrow 118

measurement, body types 57–9

membership, clubs 10–11

minimum level of fitness 22

mouth-to mouth ventilation (MMV) 92

muscles 7, 132–39

    contractions 30–1

    endurance 15, 21, 28–9, 138

    measurement 58

    strength 15, 21, 27, 138

    tone 137

O

obesity 54

observations 140–6

optimum weight 53

origins, muscles 134

ossification 116–17

osteoblasts 116–17

osteoclasts 116–17

outdoor activities 78–80

overload 21, 24

P

PEPs *see* personal exercise programmes

perfect model 145–6

performance 14, 20, 62–5, 140–55

personal exercise programmes (PEPs)
    25–9

pivot joints 125, 128

planning 151–2

plate bones 119

posture 137

presentation 72

principles, training 20–45

pulmonary circuits 96–7

push-ups 28

R

records 143–4, 149

recovery 92, 101

referees 74, 154

repetitions 32–3

respiratory system 104–11

rest, ice, compression, elevate (RICE)
    86–7

resuscitation 92

reversibility 22, 24

RICE *see* rest, ice, compression, elevate

risk assessment 68

rules 74, 141

S

safety 68–83, 91

septum 96–7

shock 90

short bones 119–20, 122

sit and reach 29

sit-ups 28

skeleton 112–13, 120

skills 15–19, 82, 141–2, 145

slow twitch muscle fibres 136

smoking 60

somatotypes 55–9

speed play 40–1

spongy bone 117–18

spotters 36

sprains 87

strength 15, 21, 27, 138

stress 7, 9

stretches 81

swimming 78

synovial joints 125–28

systematic training 20

systemic circuits 96–7

T

target zones 21–2

techniques 68–9

tendons 126–7

tennis elbow 87

tests 25–9, 65–7

throwing cages 69

tone, muscles 137

training 20–45, 111, 152–3

U

unconsciousness 90–1

V

valves 96–7

vena cava 96–7

venues 75

vertebrae 121

vertical jump tests 27

VO_2 maximum 21, 25, 26, 108

W

warming up 69, 81–2

weather reports 80

weight 34–7, 52–4

Y

yellow bone marrow 118